★ 1 All-Star

Workbook

Linda Lee ★ Stephen Sloan ★
Grace Tanaka ★ Shirley Velasco

Workbook by Kristin Sherman

 **McGraw-Hill
ESL/ELT**

All-Star 1 Workbook

Published by McGraw-Hill ESL/ELT, a business unit of The McGraw-Hill Companies, Inc. 1221 Avenue of the Americas, New York, NY 10020. Copyright © 2005 by The McGraw-Hill Companies, Inc. All rights reserved. No part of this publication may be reproduced or distributed in any form or by any means, or stored in a database or retrieval system, without the prior written consent of The McGraw-Hill Companies, Inc., including, but not limited to, in any network or other electronic storage or transmission, or broadcast for distance learning.

ISBN 0-07-284665-8

Editorial director: Tina B. Carver
Executive editor: Erik Gundersen
Director of sales and marketing: Thomas P. Dare
Developmental editors: Jennifer Monaghan, Mari Vargo
Editorial assistant: David Averbach
Production manager: Juanita Thompson
Interior designer: Wee Design Group
Cover designer: Wee Design Group
Art: Andrew Lange, NETS/Carlos Sanchis
Photo Credits: All photos are courtesy of Getty Images Royalty-Free Collection with the exception of the following: Page 125 Myrleen Ferguson Cate/PhotoEdit; Page 127 Mark Douet/Getty Images.

McGraw-Hill ESL/ELT

All-Star is a four-level, standards-based series for English learners featuring a picture-dictionary approach to vocabulary building. "Big picture" scenes in each unit provide springboards to a wealth of activities developing all of the language skills. Each *All-Star* Workbook unit provides 14 pages of supplementary exercises for its corresponding Student Book unit. The Workbook activities offer students further practice in developing the language, vocabulary, and life-skill competencies taught in the Student Book. Answers to the Workbook activities are available in the Teacher's Edition.

Features

★ **Wide range of exercises** can be used by students working independently or in groups, in the classroom, with a tutor, or at home. Each lesson includes at least one activity which allows students to interact, usually by asking and answering questions.

★ **Alternate application lessons** complement the Student Book application lesson, inviting students to tackle work, family, and/or community extension activities in each unit. Each application lesson concludes with a *Take It Outside* activity, encouraging students to use the language skills they've learned in the unit to interact with others outside of the classroom.

★ **Student Book page references** at the top of each Workbook page show how the two components support one another.

★ **Practice tests** at the end of each unit provide practice answering multiple-choice questions such as those found on the CASAS tests. Students are invited to chart their progress on these tests on a bar graph on the inside back cover.

★ **Spotlight: Grammar** lessons appear at the end of every other unit, offering supplementary grammar practice.

★ **Crossword puzzles and word searches** reinforce unit vocabulary.

Alternate Application Lessons (work, family, community)

Equipped for the Future (EFF) is a set of standards for adult literacy and lifelong learning, developed by The National Institute for Literacy (www.nifl.gov). The organizing principle of EFF is that adults assume responsibilities in three major areas of life — as workers, as parents, and as citizens. These three areas of focus are called "role maps" in the EFF documentation.

Lesson 6 in each unit of the Student Book provides a real-life application relating to one of the learners' roles. The Workbook includes two lessons, each of which addresses the other roles. This allows you, as the teacher, to customize the unit to meet the needs of your students. You can teach any or all of the application lessons in class. For example, if all your students work, you may choose to focus on the work applications. If your students have diverse interests and needs, you may have them work in small groups on different applications. If your program provides many hours of classroom time each week, you have enough material to cover all three roles.

Contents

Unit 4 Calendars

Unit 5 Clothing

Unit 6 Food

Unit 10 Work

LESSON

Where are you from?

A Write the missing letters of the countries.

China	Vietnam	Somalia	France	Morocco
Haiti	Brazil	✓ Colombia	Canada	Mexico

1. C o l _o_ _m_ b i a

2. S o __ a l __ a

3. H __ i __ i

4. __ a n __ d __

5. C h __ n __

6. B r a __ __ __

7. __ __ a n c e

8. M __ x __ c __

9. __ i __ t n __ m

10. M o __ __ c __ o

Write the name of one more country. _____

B Complete the sentences. Write *am, are,* or *is.*

1. Nicoletta ___is___ from Italy.

2. They _____ from China.

3. He _____ from Russia.

4. I _____ from England.

5. We _____ from Japan.

6. She _____ from India.

7. You _____ from Congo.

8. Ken and I _____ from Korea.

9. Paul and Henry _____ from Haiti.

10. You and Ali _____ from Morocco.

11. Eva _____ from Mexico.

am	are	is

C Write the sentences with *you, we, they, he, she,* or *it.*

1. Victor and Carlos are from Mexico.
   They are from Mexico.

2. You and Sonia are from Brazil.
   _____

3. Tanya is from Haiti.
   _____

4. Laura and I are from Colombia.
   _____

5. George is from China.
   _____

6. Martha and Elizabeth are from Canada.
   _____

7. Brazil is in South America.
   _____

you	we	they
he	she	it

D Match the questions and answers.

Questions

1. _____ Where are Sandra and Juan from?
2. _____ Where are you from?
3. _____ Where is Victor from?
4. _____ Where are you and Tien from?
5. _____ Where is Marie Claire from?
6. ___d___ Where is your teacher from?

Answers

a. She's from France.
b. They're from Mexico.
c. We're from Vietnam.
d. She's from the United States.
e. He's from Colombia.
f. I'm from Somalia.

E Write the contractions.

1. he is   _____he's_____
2. I am   _____
3. they are   _____
4. she is   _____
5. we are   _____
6. you are   _____

| I'm |
| you're |
| we're |
| he's |
| she's |
| it's |
| they're |

LESSON 2

Where's your notebook?

A Write the words under the pictures.

book   chair   clock   computer   map   table

_____

_____

_____

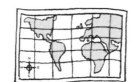

_____

_____

_____

B Circle the correct answer.

EXAMPLE: Where's the desk?

　Ⓐ It's on the floor.　　B. It's on the wall.　　C. It's on the table.

1. Where's the clock?

　A. It's on the floor.　　B. It's on the wall.　　C. It's on the table.

2. Where's the table?

　A. It's on the floor.　　B. It's on the wall.　　C. It's on the table.

3. Where's the computer?

　A. It's on the floor.　　B. It's on the wall.　　C. It's on the table.

4. Where's the map?

　A. It's on the floor.　　B. It's on the wall.　　C. It's on the table.

5. Where's the book?

　A. It's on the floor.　　B. It's on the wall.　　C. It's on the table.

C Write 5 things you have in your house.

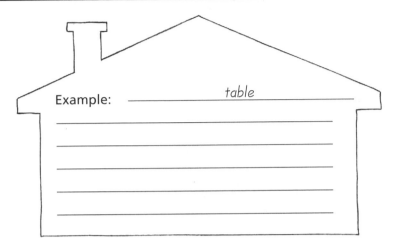

Example: _____ _table_

D Match the questions and answers.

| my | your | his | her | our | their |

Questions

1. __b__ Where's my pen?
2. _____ Where's Victor's book?
3. _____ Where's Akiko's notebook?
4. _____ Where's Sam's and my teacher?
5. _____ Where's your calendar?
6. _____ Where's Ahmed's desk?

Answers

a. His desk is on the floor.
b. Your pen is on the desk.
c. My calendar is on the wall.
d. Our teacher is in the classroom.
e. His book is on the table.
f. Her notebook is on the chair.

E Answer the questions.

1. Where is your book? _____

2. Where is your teacher? _____

3. Where is your clock? _____

4. Where is your pencil? _____

Read page 6.

A Match the instructions to the pictures. Write the number on the line.

Students,
Sit down. ____5____
Take out a piece of paper and a pencil. _____
Open your book to page 9. _____
Write your name on the piece of paper. _____
Listen to the words I say. _____
Write the words on the piece of paper. _____

1.

2.

3.

4.

5.

6.

B Check the instructions the teacher writes on the board in Activity A.

EXAMPLE:

☑ Sit down.

❑ 1. Open your book to page 9.

❑ 2. Read page 10.

❑ 3. Close the window.

❑ 4. Take out a piece of paper and a pencil.

❑ 5. Repeat the words.

❑ 6. Write your name on the piece of paper.

❑ 7. Write the words on a piece of paper.

❑ 8. Ask a partner.

❑ 9. Go to the board.

❑ 10. Listen to the words I say.

C Check the things that you can take out.

❑ 1. book

❑ 2. pen

❑ 3. pencil

❑ 4. words

❑ 5. piece of paper

❑ 6. door

❑ 7. notebook

❑ 8. hand

D Write 3 instructions your teacher says in the classroom.

EXAMPLE: _____*Take out a piece of paper.*_____

1. _____

2. _____

3. _____

E Write the numbers as words.

EXAMPLE: 10 __*ten*__

2 _____   6 _____

7 _____   4 _____

9 _____   3 _____

0 _____   1 _____

8 _____   5 _____

F Write the missing words.

EXAMPLE: six, __*seven*__, eight

1. one, two, _____

2. four, _____, six

3. nine, _____, eleven

4. seven, _____, nine

5. _____, seven, eight

G Circle the correct answer.

1. Open your book to _____ 8.

   Ⓐ page   B. board

2. Write your name on a piece of _____.

   A. pencil   B. paper

3. Close the _____.

   A. window   B. words

4. Ask _____.

   A. the board   B. a classmate

7

Application Forms

A Make words from the letters.

address	city ✓	birthplace	gender	female
male	street	state	single	married

EXAMPLE: tcyi   _____ *city* _____

1. deerng   _____
2. mlefea   _____
3. tteres   _____
4. glensi   _____
5. dsdsrae   _____

B Complete the form with your information.

Application Form
(PLEASE PRINT)

_____   _____   _____
First Name   Middle Name   Last Name

ADDRESS: _____
       Street   City   State   Zip Code

TELEPHONE NUMBER: (_____) – _____
       AREA CODE

BIRTHPLACE: _____

GENDER: ☐ Male   ☐ Female

MARITAL STATUS: ☐ Single   ☐ Married   ☐ Divorced

OCCUPATION: _____

C Read the story. Match the information.

Cindy's last name is Johnson. Her address is 451 North Street, Boise, Idaho. Her telephone number is (208) 555-4872. She is single. Cindy is a bus driver. Her birthplace is Seattle, Washington.

Information Words

1. birthplace
2. address
3. area code
4. occupation
5. marital status
6. last name

Information About Cindy

a. Johnson
b. single
c. Seattle, Washington
d. 208
e. 451 North Street, Boise, Idaho
f. bus driver

D Write the punctuation marks.

1. Where are you from?
2. I am from Hanoi Vietnam
3. What's the teacher's name
4. Her name is Susan Foster
5. What is his birthplace
6. His birthplace is Guadalajara Mexico

. , ?

E Write the sentences from Activity D in the correct place in the chart.

QUESTIONS (?)	ANSWERS (.)
1. Where are you from?	

F Read the story. Complete the sentences.

My teacher is from Houston, Texas. Her name is Rosa Lynch. She is married. Her address is 122 4th Street in Charlotte, North Carolina. The zip code is 28204. She is a teacher at the Davis Middle School. I am a student in her class.

1. The teacher's name is _____.
2. Her birthplace is _____.
3. Her city is _____.
4. Her zip code is _____.
5. Her address is _____.

She needs 10 pencils.

Luis is in grade 1.

Ling is in grade 10.

West Elementary School	Grades 1–5
South Middle School	Grades 6–8
North High School	Grades 9–12

Kristina is in grade 6.

A Look at the box above. Write the names of the schools.

1. Luis is a student at _____ _____ School.

2. Ling is a student at _____ _____ School.

3. Kristina is a student at _____ _____ School.

B Learn new words. Find and circle these words in the reading.

list	grade	binder	ruler	eraser	child

South Middle School
Grades 6–8
58 Elm Street
Charlotte, North Carolina

Parents: Read the list of school supplies for your child.

Grade 6:   Notebooks (2)   Binder (1)
                Pens (4)   Erasers (2)
                Pencils (9)   Paper

Grade 7:   Notebooks (3)   Binder (1)
                Pens (4)   Erasers (2)
                Pencils (10)   Paper
                Ruler (1)

Grade 8:   Notebooks (4)   Binders (2)
                Pens (5)   Erasers (3)
                Pencils (11)   Paper
                Ruler (1)

C Write the numbers.

1. Grade 8, erasers: _____3_____
2. Grade 6, notebooks: _____
3. Grade 8, notebooks: _____
4. Grade 7, pencils: _____
5. Grade 8, binders: _____
6. Grade 7, ruler: _____

D Answer the questions.

1. A: What is the name of the school?
   B: _____ South Middle School _____

2. A: What is the address for South Middle School?
   B: _____

3. A: What city is South Middle School in?
   B: _____

4. A: What grades are in the North High School?
   B: _____

5. A: What school is grade 3 in?
   B: _____

E Read the sentences. Write the numbers.

1. Abraham Beyene is in grade 7. He needs _____ notebooks.
2. Soon Yi Park is in grade 8. She needs _____ binders.
3. Kristina Hallek is in grade 6. She needs _____ pens.
4. Claudio Rivera is in grade 6. He needs _____ pencils.
5. Zana Daka is in grade 8. She needs _____ erasers.

★ ★

TAKE IT OUTSIDE: Interview a family member, friend, or coworker. Ask the questions.
Write the answers.

What is your child's name?	What grade is your child in?	What are the school supplies your child needs?
Example: Luis	grade 1	pencils, paper, notebook

★ ★

COMMUNITY
LESSON

What's your address?

Keiko writes and
sends the letter.

A Learn new words. Find and underline these words.

send/sends	receive/receives	letter
return address	stamp	envelope

Dear Mrs. Lynch,

    I am a student at Central
Community College. I am from Japan. I
am also a teacher. I can practice English
with your students. I can teach your
students to write their names in
Japanese. My telephone number is
(704) 555–0123.

Sincerely,
Keiko Ishikawa

letter

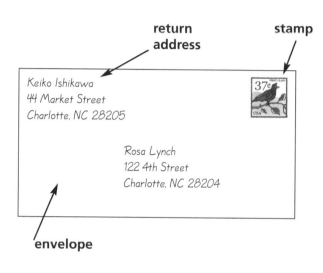

**return
address**

stamp

Keiko Ishikawa
44 Market Street
Charlotte, NC 28205

Rosa Lynch
122 4th Street
Charlotte, NC 28204

envelope

The letter goes to
Rosa Lynch. Rosa
receives the letter.

B Answer the questions.

1. Who writes the letter? _____

2. Who reads the letter? _____

3. What is Keiko's last name? _____

4. What is Mrs. Lynch's first name? _____

5. What is Keiko's address? _____

C Check *yes* or *no* about the letter and the envelope.

1. Keiko writes the letter. ☑ yes ☐ no

2. Rosa's address is 44 Market Street. ☐ yes ☐ no

3. Keiko is from Japan. ☐ yes ☐ no

4. Rosa's city is Charlotte. ☐ yes ☐ no

5. Keiko's last name is Lynch. ☐ yes ☐ no

6. Mrs. Lynch's first name is Rosa. ☐ yes ☐ no

D Write your name and address on the envelope. Write the new words on the lines.

| letter | envelope | stamp | return address |

_____

> Dear Mrs. Lynch,
>
> I am a student. My name is . . .
>
> _____
>
> _____
>
> _____

Rosa Lynch
122 4th Street
Charlotte, NC 28204

★ ★

TAKE IT OUTSIDE: Ask a family member, friend, or coworker for his or her name and address. Write it on the envelope. Write your name and address on the envelope.

★ ALTERNATE APPLICATION ★ ★ ★ ★ ★ Sending Letters ★ ★ ★ ★ ★

Practice Test

DIRECTIONS: Answer the questions. Use the Answer Sheet.

1. What is her <u>telephone number</u>?
   A. (617) 555-5643
   B. 555-89-7723
   C. 544 Martindale Street
   D. February 1, 1956

2. What is my <u>address</u>?
   A. (617) 555-5643
   B. 555-89-7723
   C. 544 Martindale Street
   D. February 1, 1956

3. What is Susan's <u>city</u>?
   A. Chicago
   B. Mexico
   C. 22903
   D. 212

4. What is Leo's <u>marital status</u>?
   A. male
   B. single
   C. gender
   D. teacher

5. What is Lana's <u>gender</u>?
   A. married
   B. nurse
   C. address
   D. female

6. What thing opens and closes?
   A. a door
   B. a map
   C. a floor
   D. a partner

7. What do you read?
   A. a window
   B. a book
   C. a teacher
   D. a pen

8. What do you take out?
   A. a word
   B. a hand
   C. a piece of paper
   D. a window

ANSWER SHEET

	A	B	C	D
1	Ⓐ	Ⓑ	Ⓒ	Ⓓ
2	Ⓐ	Ⓑ	Ⓒ	Ⓓ
3	Ⓐ	Ⓑ	Ⓒ	Ⓓ
4	Ⓐ	Ⓑ	Ⓒ	Ⓓ
5	Ⓐ	Ⓑ	Ⓒ	Ⓓ
6	Ⓐ	Ⓑ	Ⓒ	Ⓓ
7	Ⓐ	Ⓑ	Ⓒ	Ⓓ
8	Ⓐ	Ⓑ	Ⓒ	Ⓓ
9	Ⓐ	Ⓑ	Ⓒ	Ⓓ
10	Ⓐ	Ⓑ	Ⓒ	Ⓓ

DIRECTIONS: Look at the envelope to answer the next 2 questions. Use the Answer Sheet on page 14.

Maurice Nzuzi
1981 Tenth Street
Madison, WI 53701

Sandra Escobar
488 Hampshire Street
Cambridge, MA 01622

9. Who sends the letter?

   A. Sandra Escobar

   B. Sandra Cambridge

   C. Maurice Nzuzi

   D. Madison, WI

10. Who does the letter go to?

   A. Sandra Escobar

   B. Sandra Cambridge

   C. Maurice Nzuzi

   D. Madison, WI

HOW DID YOU DO? Count the number of correct answers on your answer sheet. Record this number in the bar graph on the inside back cover.

Spotlight: Grammar

SIMPLE PRESENT OF *BE*		
I **am** a student. **am not** a teacher.	You We They **are** single. **are not** married.	He She It **is** from China. **is not** from Japan.

CONTRACTIONS	
I'm	I'm not
you're	you aren't
we're	we aren't
they're	they aren't
he's	he isn't
she's	she isn't
it's	it isn't
Fatima's	Fatima isn't

A Complete the story. Use words from the box.

My name _____ Patricia. I _____ from Ghana. My teacher

_____ from the United States. Her name _____ Monica Timmons.

_____ married. There _____ 22 students in my class.

am	is
are	I'm
you're	he's
she's	we're
they're	aren't
isn't	

Five students _____ from Somalia, and ten _____ from

Mexico. Six students _____ Chinese. They _____ from

Beijing. _____ the only student from Ghana. We _____ all in

English class.

B Read the story again. Circle the correct words.

1. Monica Timmons (is / isn't) the teacher.
2. Patricia (is / isn't) a student.
3. She (is / isn't) married.
4. Ten students (are / aren't) from Mexico.
5. Patricia (is / isn't) from Somalia.
6. Monica Timmons (is / isn't) from Ghana.

16

C Rewrite the words. Use contractions.

1. I am _____
2. you are _____
3. we are _____
4. he is _____
5. it is _____
6. she is _____
7. they are _____

8. you are not _____
9. he is not _____
10. I am not _____
11. they are not _____
12. she is not _____
13. it is not _____
14. we are not _____

POSSESSIVE ADJECTIVES: *MY, YOUR, OUR, THEIR, HIS, HER*

my book　　**your** book　　**our** book　　**their** book　　**her** book　　**his** book

POSSESSIVES OF NAMES

John's book is here.
Tina's book is on the table.
Mr. Campos's book is on the desk.

John and Tina's teacher is Mr. Campos.
Andy's address is on the application form.
Ms. Jones's zip code is 94704.

D Write the possessive adjectives.

I _____
you _____
she _____

he _____
we _____
they _____

E Circle the correct answer.

1. Betty is a student. _____ teacher is Mrs. Smith.

   A. Her   B. Their   C. My

2. Liu and Akiko live in Richmond. _____ address is 32 Market Street.

   A. Her   B. Their   C. My

3. Ursula and I live near the school. _____ house is on Gray Street.

   A. My   B. Their   C. Our

4. George is a teacher. _____ last name is Matthews.

   A. Her   B. His   C. My

5. I'm not married. _____ marital status is single.

   A. Your   B. Their   C. My

Where's the post office?

A Write the words next to the pictures.

park	gas station	school	supermarket

1. _____

2. _____

3. _____

4. _____

B Complete the sentences.

1. There is a _____*police station*_____ on Main Street.

2. There is a _____ on Baxter Street.

3. There is a _____ on Elm Street.

4. There is a _____ on Madison Street.

5. There is a _____ on Cedar Park Street.

G-16

M
A
R
S
H
V
I
L
L
E

MARSHVILLE, CITY OF —
Cedar Park Elementary School
  100 Cedar Park Street.............(703) 555-1023
Community Center
  201 Elm Street........................(703) 555-5289
Fire Station
  1300 Madison Street...............(703) 555-9002
Library
  251 Baxter Street....................(703) 555-7700
Police Station
  1250 Main Street.....................(703) 555-8990

UNITED STATES GOVERNMENT
Post Office
  1100 State Street.....................(703) 555-4563

C Match the questions and answers.

Questions

1. __*b*__ Where's the post office?

2. _____ Where's the police station?

3. _____ Where's the library?

4. _____ Where's the fire station?

5. _____ Where's the community center?

6. _____ Where's the elementary school?

Answers

a. It's on Main Street.

b. It's on State Street.

c. It's on Cedar Park Street.

d. It's on Madison Street.

e. It's on Baxter Street.

f. It's on Elm Street.

D Write the words in the correct order.

There is/There are

1. seven restaurants/There are/in Marshville _____ *There are seven restaurants in Marshville.* _____
2. on Main Street/one drugstore/There is _____
3. There is/on Baxter Street/one library _____
4. ten gas stations/There are/in my city _____
5. There are/in town/two police stations _____
6. three laundromats/in my city/There are _____

E Circle the correct answer.

1. Where's the community center?

   Ⓐ It's on Elizabeth Avenue.   B. Yes, it is.

2. What's the phone number?

   A. 555-4431   B. It's on Main Street.

3. What's the address?

   A. I'm not sure.   B. Thanks.

4. Thanks.

   A. Yes, it is   B. You're welcome.

F Answer the questions about your town or city.

1. Where's your post office? _____
2. Where's your fire station? _____
3. Where's your library? _____
4. Where's your police station? _____

G Write 2 sentences about your town or city. Begin with *There is* or *There are*. . .

_____

_____

_____

LESSON

It's next to the drugstore.

A Complete the sentences.

```
PARKING GARAGE
BANK    POST    FIRE STATION    POLICE
        OFFICE                  STATION
        THIRD STREET
LIBRARY  GAS      MOVIE    DRUGSTORE
   STATE STATION  THEATER
   STREET LAUNDROMAT
RESTAURANT
                    PARK
PARK    SUPER
ELEMENTARY MARKET
SCHOOL
                HOSPITAL
```

| next to | between | in back of |
| across from | on the corner of | |

1. The bank is _____ the post office.

2. The drugstore is _____ the police station.

3. The park is _____ the hospital.

4. The movie theater is _____ the gas station and the drugstore.

5. The library is _____ Third Street and State Street.

B Answer the questions. Write *Yes, there is* or *No, there isn't*.

EXAMPLE: Is there a supermarket on State Street?   *Yes, there is.*

1. Is there a restaurant on State Street?   _____

2. Is there a gas station next to the bank?   _____

3. Is there a movie theater on Third Street?   _____

4. Is there a school across from the post office?   _____

5. Is there a drugstore next to the bank?   _____

| Yes, there is./ |
| No, there isn't. |

C Complete the sentences.

EXAMPLE: The _____*gas station*_____ is across State Street from the library.

1. The fire station is between the post office and the _____.

2. The park is in back of the _____.

3. The _____ is next to the school.

4. The gas station is on the corner of _____ and _____ streets.

5. The _____ is next to the laundromat.

20

D Write the answers. Use the information in Activity A.

1. A: Excuse me. Where's the library?

   B: _____

2. A: Is that on Third Street?

   B: _____

3. A: Thanks.

   B: _____

E Circle 6 places near or in Ballenbrook Estates.

F Write the places in the correct place in the chart.

NEAR BALLENBROOK ESTATES	IN BALLENBROOK ESTATES
schools	community center

BALLENBROOK ESTATES

**VISIT OUR NEW HOMES
STARTING IN THE 150s**

Near excellent schools, supermarkets, and restaurants Ballenbrook Estates has its own community center, post office, and laundromat.

CALL 555-7892 TODAY.

G Complete the questions. Write *Is there* or *Are there*. Then answer the questions.

1. A: _____ a movie theater near your home?

   B: _____ .

2. A: _____ any drugstores in your town?

   B: _____ .

> **Is there/Are there**
> Yes, there is.
> No, there isn't.
> Yes, there are.
> No, there aren't.

H Answer the questions about you.

1. Who sits in front of you?   _____

2. Who sits in back of you?   _____

3. Who sits next to you?   _____

LESSON

Is there an ATM around here?

A Write the words next to the signs.

car	pay phone	ATM	police	bus stop
mailbox	parking	laundromat	a stop light	

1. _____

2. _____

3. _____

4. _____

5. _____

6. _____

7. _____

8. _____

9. _____

B Put the conversation in order. Number the sentences from first (1) to last (4).

_____ No problem.

_____ Excuse me. Is there a pay phone around here?

_____ Yes, there's one on Trade Street. It's in front of the supermarket.

_____ Thanks a lot.

C Look at the picture. Answer the questions. Write *Yes, there is* or *No, there isn't*.

1. Is there a pay phone in the post office?

   _____

2. Is there parking next to the supermarket?

   _____

3. Is there a bus stop on Third Street?

   _____

Yes, there is./No, there isn't.

POST OFFICE

SUPERMARKET

DRUGSTORE

THIRD STREET

LIBRARY

D Match the questions and answers.

Questions	Answers
1. _____ Is there a mailbox near here?	a. Yes, there are. In front of the bank.
2. _____ Where's the post office?	b. It's next to the police station.
3. _____ What's the phone number?	c. That's right.
4. _____ Next to the library?	d. 555-4092
5. _____ Are there any pay phones on this street?	e. Yes, there is.

E Look at the picture. Write *There is* or *There are* and the number.

1. _____*There is one*_____ gas station.

2. _____ ATMs.

3. _____ pay phones.

4. _____ bus stop.

5. _____ supermarket.

6. _____ mailbox.

There is/There are

F Answer the questions about your town or city.

1. Is there a pay phone near your classroom?

   _____

2. Where's the bus stop?

   _____

3. Is there a laundromat near your home?

   _____

4. Is there a hospital on your street?

   _____

5. Is there an ATM near your home?

   _____

Maps

A Circle the correct answer and write the names of the towns on the lines.

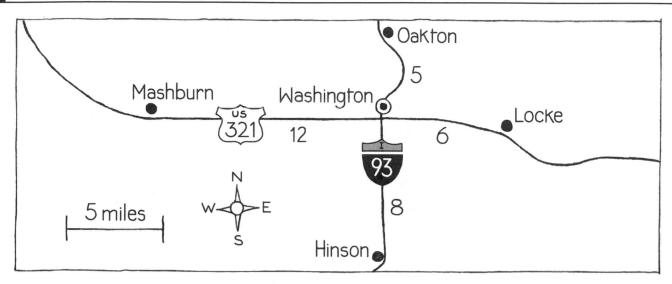

1. _____ is north of Washington.   A. Hinson   B. Oakton

2. _____ is west of Washington.   A. Hinson   B. Mashburn

3. _____ is south of Washington.   A. Hinson   B. Locke

4. Washington is _____ of Locke.   A. west   B. south

5. Washington is _____ of Oakton.   A. north   B. south

6. Oakton is _____ of Washington.   A. west   B. north

B Answer the questions.

1. What town is east of Washington?   _____

2. What towns are east of Mashburn on Hwy 321?   _____

3. What towns are north of Hinson on I-93?   _____

4. What town is west of Washington?   _____

5. What town is between Hinson and Oakton?   _____

C Complete the sentences.

1. It is ___5___ miles from Washington to Oakton.

2. Hinson is _____ miles from Washington.

3. There are _____ miles between Washington and Mashburn.

4. Locke is _____ miles from Washington.

5. There are _____ miles between Washington and Oakton.

6. There are _____ miles between Hinson and Washington.

D Write the math symbols.

+ plus (and)	> is more than	= equals	– minus	< is less than
1 + 2 = 3	6 > 5		3 – 2 = 1	8 < 9

1. How many miles is it from Washington to Oakton and back?   5 _+_ 5 _=_ 10

2. How many miles is it from Oakton to Hinson?   5 ___ 8 ___ 13

3. How many miles is it from Mashburn to Locke?   12 ___ 6 ___ 18

4. Is Oakton or Hinson more miles from Washington?   5 ___ 8

5. How many miles is it from Washington to Locke and back?   6 ___ 6 ___ 12

6. Sam's address is 581 Hwy 321. It is 2 miles west of Washington, between Washington and Mashburn. How many miles is it from Sam's address to Mashburn?   12 ___ 2 ___ 10

E Answer the questions about your city or town.

1. How many miles is it from your home to school?   _____

2. What town is north of your city or town?   _____

3. What state do you live in?   _____

4. What state is east of your state?   _____

F Write about you.

I live in the town/city of _____. It is in the state of _____.
The capital of the state is _____. My state is next to _____.

FAMILY LESSON

Where's the nurse's office?

A Learn new words. Find and circle these words in the map.

| gym | cafeteria | main office | nurse's office | playground |

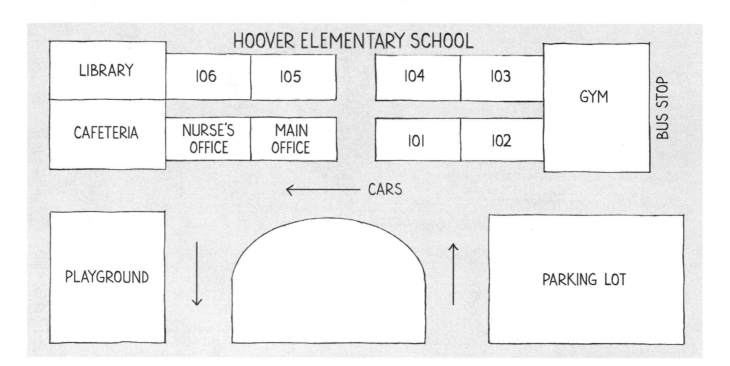

B Complete the sentences.

| next to | between | across from | in front of | near |

1. The bus stop is _____ the gym.

2. Room 102 is _____ Room 101.

3. The cafeteria is _____ the library.

4. Room 105 is _____ the main office.

5. The nurse's office is _____ the cafeteria and the main office.

C Match the questions and answers.

Questions	Answers
1. _f_ Where's the nurse's office?	a. It's across from the cafeteria.
2. ___ Where's the library?	b. It's in back of the cafeteria.
3. ___ Where's the cafeteria?	c. It's across from room 104.
4. ___ Where's room 101?	d. It's near the gym.
5. ___ Where's the bus stop?	e. It's next to the nurse's office.
6. ___ Where's the playground?	f. It's next to the main office.

D Answer the questions.

1. Where's the bus stop?   _It's near the gym._
2. Where's the playground?   _____
3. Where's the nurse's office?   _____
4. Where's the main office?   _____
5. Where's the parking lot?   _____
6. Where's room 106?   _____

E Check *yes* or *no* about the picture on page 26.

1. There is a bus stop.   ❑ yes   ❑ no
2. The cafeteria is next to the gym.   ❑ yes   ❑ no
3. There are six classrooms.   ❑ yes   ❑ no
4. The playground is in the school.   ❑ yes   ❑ no
5. There are two libraries.   ❑ yes   ❑ no

★ ★

TAKE IT OUTSIDE: Interview a family member, friend, or coworker.

What is the name of your child's school? _____

Do your children go on the bus or in the car? _____

★ ★

How many miles do you go?

A Learn new words. Find and circle these words in the story.

| drive/drives | work/works | odometer | mileage log |

Marco is a bus driver. His last name is Santori. He drives a school bus. He works at Hoover Elementary School in Washington. The school is on Highway 321. He goes to other cities and to the gas station in the bus. He reads the odometer. He writes the miles he drives every day on a mileage log. He writes his name on the mileage log, too.

B Complete the sentences. Use words from the story.

1. Marco is a _____.
2. He works at _____.
3. He writes the miles on a _____.
4. He drives to other _____ and to the _____.
5. The school is on _____.

MILEAGE LOG					
DATE	DESTINATION AND REASON	STARTING ODOMETER	ENDING ODOMETER	MILES	DRIVER
1/19	Hoover School to town of Locke and back (morning run)	8925.0	8935.0	10.0	Marco Santori
1/19	Hoover School to gas station for gas and back	8935.0	8938.0	3.0	Marco Santori
1/19	Hoover School to town of Locke and back (afternoon run)	8938.0	8948.0	10.0	Marco Santori

C Answer the questions about Marco.

1. What is Marco's occupation? _____

2. Where does he work? _____

3. How many miles is it from school to the gas station? _____

4. How many miles is it from the school to the town of Locke and back?

   _____

5. What is Marco's last name? _____

6. Where is the school? _____

D Complete the table with information about where you go today.

DATE	DESTINATION AND REASON	NUMBER OF MILES
3/15	Home to school and back	6

E Answer the questions.

1. Where do you go today? _____

2. How many miles is it? _____

F Write a story about yourself.

I am a _____. My last name is _____. I go to school at _____

in _____. The school is on _____. I go to _____, too.

★ ★

TAKE IT OUTSIDE: If your workplace uses a mileage sheet, get a copy. If not, make one.

Interview a family member, friend, or coworker about his or her trips each day. Ask the questions. Write the answers.

Where do you go every day? _____

How many miles do you go every day? _____

★ ★

Practice Test

DIRECTIONS: Look at the map to answer the next 5 questions. Use the Answer Sheet.

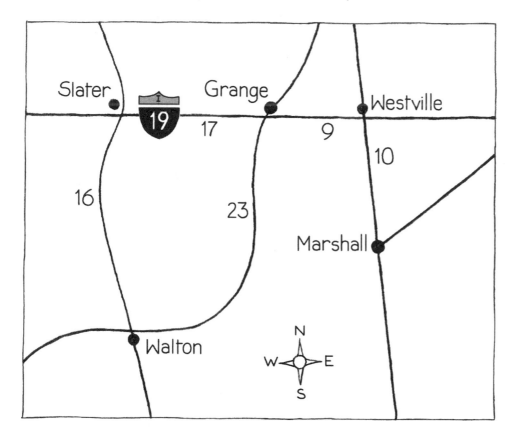

ANSWER SHEET

1. (A) (B) (C) (D)
2. (A) (B) (C) (D)
3. (A) (B) (C) (D)
4. (A) (B) (C) (D)
5. (A) (B) (C) (D)
6. (A) (B) (C) (D)
7. (A) (B) (C) (D)
8. (A) (B) (C) (D)
9. (A) (B) (C) (D)
10. (A) (B) (C) (D)

1. How far is it from Walton to Grange?

   A. 17 miles　　　B. 9 miles　　　C. 23 miles　　　D. 32 miles

2. How far is it from Slater to Grange and back?

   A. 17 miles　　　B. 34 miles　　　C. 26 miles　　　D. 32 miles

3. What direction is Westville from Marshall?

   A. north　　　B. west　　　C. south　　　D. east

4. What city is west of Grange on I-19?

   A. Slater　　　B. Walton　　　C. Westville　　　D. Marshall

5. What city is east of Grange on I-19?

   A. Slater　　　B. Walton　　　C. Westville　　　D. Marshall

DIRECTIONS: Look at the map to answer the next 5 questions. Use the Answer Sheet on page 30.

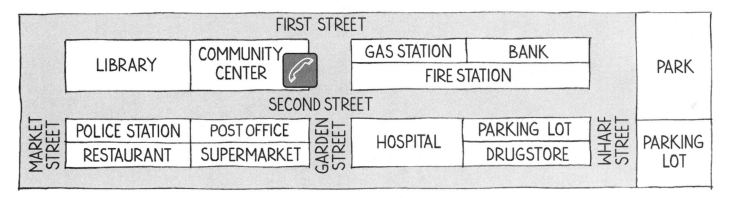

6. Where is the bank?

   A. It's on First Street.

   B. It's on Market Street.

   C. It's on Garden Street.

   D. It's on Second Street.

7. Where is the supermarket?

   A. It's next to the bank.

   B. It's next to the library.

   C. It's next to the restaurant.

   D. It's next to the hospital.

8. Where is the fire station?

   A. It's on First Street.

   B. It's across from the hospital.

   C. It's next to the drugstore.

   D. It's between the gas station and the bank.

9. Which sentence is correct?

   A. The community center is across from the library.

   B. There are three parking lots.

   C. There are two restaurants.

   D. The post office is on the corner of Second Street and Garden Street.

10. Where is a pay phone?

    A. In the police station.

    B. In the parking lot next to the park.

    C. In the community center.

    D. In back of the hospital.

HOW DID YOU DO? Count the number of correct answers on your answer sheet. Record this number in the bar graph on the inside back cover.

What time is it?

A Write the times below the clocks.

1. ___2:00___   2. _____   3. _____   4. _____   5. _____

6. _____   7. _____   8. _____   9. _____   10. _____

B Write the numbers another way.

EXAMPLE: 45 ___forty-five___   ___12___ twelve

1. 15   _____   6. _____   thirty-three

2. _____   forty-six   7. 52   _____

3. 17   _____   8. 35   _____

4. 32   _____   9. _____   fifty-five

5. _____   twenty-nine   10. 18   _____

C Answer the questions. Use the clocks below.

EXAMPLE: A: What time is it?   B: It's three-thirty.

             A: Is it three o'clock?   B: No, it isn't. It's three-thirty.

             A: Is it three-thirty?   B: Yes, it is.

1. A: What time is it?   B: _____.

2. A: Excuse me. What time is it?   B: _____.

3. A: Is it nine o'clock?   B: _____.

4. A: Is it seven-thirty?      B: _____.

D Answer the questions about you.

1. What time is your class? _____

2. Is your class in the morning? _____

3. Is your school open at 7:00 A.M.? _____

4. Is your school open at midnight? _____

5. Is your supermarket open at 8:00 P.M.? _____

E Complete the sentences.

in the morning	at night	minutes	noon	after
in the afternoon	before	A.M.	P.M.	in the evening

1. 8:00 A.M. is eight o'clock _____.

2. There are 60 _____ in an hour.

3. Another name for 12:00 P.M. is _____.

4. Another way to say in the morning is _____.

5. The number 15 is _____ 14.

6. The number 21 is _____ 22.

7. Some supermarkets are open _____, but more are closed.

F Complete the questions. Write *Is* or *Are*.

1. _____ your bank open in the afternoon?

2. _____ your class at night?

3. _____ drugstores open in the evening?

4. _____ supermarkets open in the morning?

5. _____ your library open at 10:00 P.M.?

is	are

2
LESSON

Is the library open on Monday?

A Find these words in the puzzle. Circle them.

~~morning~~	night
Monday	time
Thursday	computer
telephone	pen
afternoon	checkout
week	video
closed	clock
forty	desk
library	from
Wednesday	five

```
m  o  r  n  i  n  g  u  p  f  a  M
t  e  l  e  p  h  o  n  e  r  d  o
a  f  t  e  r  n  o  o  n  o  b  n
b  v  q  n  i  g  h  t  i  m  e  d
l  c  o  m  p  u  t  e  r  s  p  a
e  l  u  x  w  l  i  b  r  a  r  y
f  o  r  v  i  d  e  o  f  i  v  e
o  c  y  o  u  d  o  o  r  j  i  n
r  k  i  c  h  e  c  k  o  u  t  z
t  T  h  u  r  s  d  a  y  z  i  p
y  s  w  e  e  k  c  l  o  s  e  d
W  e  d  n  e  s  d  a  y  g  o  t
```

B Complete the sentences. Use words from the puzzle.

EXAMPLE: This unit is about ___time___ and money.

1. _____ is the day after Tuesday.

2. The day before Friday is _____.

3. The day after Sunday is _____.

4. The library is open from 10 o'clock in the _____ to 9 o'clock at _____ on Wednesday.

5. On Sundays and Thursdays the library is not open, it is _____.

C Look at the hours of the post office. Answer the questions.

> **U.S. Post Office**
> **Hours of Operation**
>
>   Sunday: **CLOSED**
>   Monday: **from 7:00** A.M. **to 5:30** P.M.
>   Tuesday: **from 7:00** A.M. **to 5:30** P.M.
> Wednesday: **from 7:00** A.M. **to 5:30** P.M.
>   Thursday: **from 7:00** A.M. **to 5:30** P.M.
>   Friday: **from 7:00** A.M. **to 4:30** P.M.
>   Saturday: **from 8:00** A.M. **to noon**

1. When is the post office open on Monday? _____ *from 7:00 A.M. to 5:30 P.M.* _____

2. Is the post office open on Saturday? _____

3. Is the post office open on Sunday? _____

4. When is the post office open on Friday? _____

5. When is the post office open on Thursday? _____

6. When is the post office open on Tuesday? _____

D Circle *yes* or *no* for each sentence.

1. The post office is open at Wednesday at noon.   (yes)   no

2. The post office is closed on Saturday at 6:00 P.M.   yes   no

3. The post office is open on Tuesday at midnight.   yes   no

4. The post office is closed on Sunday.   yes   no

5. The post office is open on Friday at 2:00 P.M.   yes   no

E Write the words in the correct order.

1. the library/When is/on Tuesday/open
   _____ *When is the library open on Tuesday?* _____

2. the supermarket/open/at midnight/Is
   _____?

3. is/at 5:00 A.M./closed/The gas station
   _____.

4. The hospital/Sunday to Saturday/is open
   _____.

5. is closed/at 6:00 P.M./The park
   _____.

3
LESSON

It's five cents.

A Put the words in order.

| < is less than | > is more than | = equals |

| dime | dollar | nickel | quarter | penny |

1. ___penny___ < 2. _____ < 3. _____ < 4. _____ < 5. _____

B Write the amounts another way.

EXAMPLE: a penny ___1¢___   ___a nickel___ 5¢

1. a quarter   _____
2. a dollar   _____
3. _____ $5.00
4. a nickel   _____
5. twenty dollars   _____
6. _____ $50.00
7. _____   10¢
8. one thousand dollars   _____

C Answer the questions.

EXAMPLE: How much is 20¢ and 30¢?   ___50¢___

1. How much is one dollar and 10 dollars?   _____
2. How much is a quarter and a nickel?   _____
3. How much is 50 dollars and 3 dollars?   _____
4. How much is a dime and a quarter?   _____
5. How much is 25¢ and 40¢?   _____
6. How much is it?   _____
7. How much is it?   _____
8. How much is it?   _____
9. How much is a penny and a nickel?   _____
10. How much is 10¢ and a nickel?   _____

How much?

6.
7.
8.

D Read the sign. Match the questions and answers.

Questions	Answers
1. How much is a new video or DVD?	a. No, it's not. It's $10 for 3 videos.
2. How much is a video game?	b. It's $4.50 for 2 evenings.
3. How much is a regular video?	c. It's $3.95 for 5 evenings.
4. Is it $4.50 for 3 evenings?	d. No, it's not. It's $4.50 for 2 evenings.
5. Is it $10 for one video?	e. It's $2.95 for 5 evenings.

E Answer the questions.

1. How much is a video at your library or video store? _____

2. How much is an overdue book at your library? _____

3. How much is this workbook? _____

How much?

LESSON 4

Checks

A Read the checks. Circle *yes* or *no*.

SUSAN KELLER
121 Beacon St.
Somerville, MA 06172   072

DATE 3/12/05

PAY TO THE
ORDER OF Movie Town Videos $ 7.90

Seven and 90/100 _____ DOLLARS

TRUE BANK
Massachusetts

MEMO videos and games   Susan Keller

⑈012345678⑈:   123⑈456 7⑈ 0072

SUSAN KELLER
121 Beacon St.
Somerville, MA 06172   073

DATE 3/13/05

PAY TO THE
ORDER OF Savemor's Supermarket $ 22.10

Twenty-two and 10/100 _____ DOLLARS

TRUE BANK
Massachusetts

MEMO food   Susan Keller

⑈012345678⑈:   123⑈456 7⑈ 0073

---

1. The check to Movie Town Videos is for $22.10	yes	(no)
2. The check to Movie Town Videos is number 072.	yes	no
3. Susan Keller writes the checks.	yes	no
4. The check for $22.10 is check number 073.	yes	no
5. The check for $7.90 is for videos and games.	yes	no
6. Susan writes a check to FoodFresh Supermarket.	yes	no
7. Susan writes a check to Movie Town Videos in February.	yes	no
8. Susan lives in True Bank, Massachusetts.	yes	no
9. Susan's zip code is 31305.	yes	no
10. Susan writes a check to Savemor's Supermarket on March 13.	yes	no

B Circle the correct answer.

1. What is the name of the supermarket?
   A. Savemor's   B. Susan Keller

2. How much is check number 072?
   A. $7.90   B. $22.10

3. What is check number 073 for?
   A. videos   B. food

4. What is Susan Keller's address?
   A. 121 Beacon St.   B. True Bank, Massachusetts

5. What is the amount of the check to Movie Town Videos?
   A. videos and games   B. $7.90

C Write the missing numbers.

1. $10.00 + $3.50 = _____
2. $4.95 + $2.95 = _____
3. $22.10 + $7.90 = _____
4. $4.00 + 95¢ = _____
5. $12.00 + $2.95 = _____

6. $10.00 – $5.00 = _____
7. $5.00 – .50 = _____
8. $1.00 – 25¢ = _____
9. $50.00 – $7.00 = _____
10. $20.00 – $12.00 = _____

D Read the chart. Write the missing numbers.

CHECK #	TO	AMOUNT	FOR	BALANCE
072	Movie Town Videos	$7.90	videos	$100.00 – $ 7.90
073	Savemor's Supermarket	$22.10	food	= $ 92.10 – $ 22.10
074	Jiffy Gas	$20.00	gas	= $ 70.00 – $ 20.00
075	Post office	$10.00	stamps	= – $ 10.00
076	Safe Drugstore	$15.00	drugs	= $ 40.00
077	Movie Theater	$15.00	tickets	

WORK

LESSON

Do you get vacation leave?

A Learn new words. Find and underline these words in the story.

full-time   salary   vacation   vacation leave   get/gets

Paul is a salesclerk. He works in a supermarket. He is a full-time worker. His salary is $10.00 an hour. He works 40 hours in a week. Paul gets vacation leave. He can go on vacation for 80 hours, or 10 working days, every year. He gets $10.00 an hour on vacation!

B Circle the correct answer.

1. What is Paul's occupation?
   A. a salesclerk   B. a cashier

2. Where is his work?
   A. at a gas station   B. in a supermarket

3. How much does he work?
   A. 10 days a year   B. 40 hours a week

4. How much is his salary?
   A. $10.00 an hour   B. $15.00 an hour

5. How much vacation leave does Paul get?
   A. $10.00 an hour   B. 10 days a year

C Complete the sentences. Use words from the story.

1. A job that is 40 hours a week is a _____ - _____ job.
2. The money you get for work is a _____.
3. When you are not at work, you are on _____.
4. In some jobs, you can go on vacation and still get money. This is _____ _____.

D Talk to Paul about his job. Match your questions and his answers.

Your Questions

1. "Where is your work?"
2. "What is your occupation?"
3. "What is the salary?"
4. "How much vacation leave do you get?"
5. "How much do you work a week?"
6. "Is that full-time?"

Paul's Answers

a. "I'm a salesclerk."
b. "I work in a supermarket."
c. "Yes, it is full-time."
d. "The salary is $10.00 an hour."
e. "I get 10 days of vacation leave."
f. "I work 40 hours a week."

E Read the information for Paul. Complete the sentences.

Employee name: **Paul Ming**	Period beginning: **07/24/04**	Period ending: **07/31/04**

Salary	Hours	Current $	Year to Date $
$10.00/hour	**40**	**$400.00**	**$12,000.00**

Vacation Leave	Balance on 7/31/04	Leave used
	6 days (48 hours)	0

1. Paul gets $_____ an hour.
2. Paul works _____ hours in the week of 7/24 – 7/31.
3. Paul gets $_____ for the week of 7/24 – 7/31.
4. There are _____ days of vacation leave for Paul on 7/31/04.

★ ★

TAKE IT OUTSIDE: Interview a family member, friend, or coworker. Ask the questions. Write the answers. Then write a paragraph.

1. What is your occupation? _____
2. Where is your work? _____
3. How much do you work a week? _____
4. Do you get vacation leave? _____

Paul is a salesclerk. He works in a supermarket. He works 40 hours a week. Paul gets vacation leave.

_____

_____

_____

★ ALTERNATE APPLICATION: Understanding Vacation Leave ★

41

Where's the hotel?

A Learn new words. Find and circle these words in the ads.

hotel	beach	car

A Room at Ocean Beach
Just for You!

Hotel Special $69 a night
August 1-15 only

- Room on the beach for two
- Near movies, stores and more
- Restaurant in hotel

Sand Castle Beach Hotel
1-800-555-3211

VACATION TIME?

Any car
Only $30 a day

Sunday–Thursday
(Ask about free miles.)

Martin Autos
1300 South Street
Ocean Beach

B Complete the sentences. Use words or numbers from the ads.

1. A place with rooms is called a _____*hotel*_____.
2. A room is $_____ a night.
3. A car is $_____ a day.
4. You drive to the beach in a _____.
5. The address for Martin Autos is _____.
6. The telephone number for Sand Castle Beach Hotel is _____.

C Check the things that are in the ads.

Sand Castle Beach Hotel

❑ address

❑ telephone number

❑ amount of money for a room

❑ name of the hotel

❑ days of the week

Martin Autos

❑ address

❑ telephone number

❑ amount of money for a car

❑ name of car company

❑ days of the week

D Read the story. Write the amounts of money.

Paul is on vacation in Ocean Beach. He drives to Ocean Beach in a car from Martin Autos. His room is at the Sand Castle Beach Hotel. How much is his room and car?

EXAMPLE: For Wednesday (1 day car + 1 night room) _____ *$99* _____

1. For Monday and Tuesday nights (2 days, 2 nights) _____

2. For Sunday to Thursday afternoon (5 days, 4 nights) _____

3. For Tuesday to Wednesday afternoon _____

4. A room for 3 nights and a car for 1 day _____

★ ★

TAKE IT OUTSIDE: Plan a vacation. Look at a map. Find an ad for a hotel. Find an ad for a car company. Talk to your family or friends. Answer the questions.

1. Where is your vacation (what city)? _____

2. Is it at the beach? _____

3. What is the name of the hotel? _____

4. How much is a room in the hotel? _____

5. What is the name of the car company? _____

6. How much is a car? _____

★ ★

Practice Test

DIRECTIONS: Circle the correct answer. Use the Answer Sheet.

1. It's one o'clock.

A.

B.

C.

D.

2. It's 3:30.

A.

B.

C.

D.

3. It's 20¢.

A. two dimes

B. two nickels

C. a dime and a nickel

D. a nickel and a penny

4. How much money is it?

A. $8.00

B. $.80

C. 8¢

D. $.08

ANSWER SHEET				
1	A	B	C	D
2	A	B	C	D
3	A	B	C	D
4	A	B	C	D
5	A	B	C	D
6	A	B	C	D
7	A	B	C	D
8	A	B	C	D
9	A	B	C	D
10	A	B	C	D

5. How much is two dimes and two dollars?

A. $2.10   B. $20.10   C. $2.02   D. $2.20

6. How much is five nickels and five dollars?

A. $25.25   B. $5.05   C. $25.05   D. $5.25

7. How much is the stamp?

A.

B.

C.

D.

44

DIRECTIONS: Look at the check to answer the next 3 questions. Use the Answer Sheet on page 44.

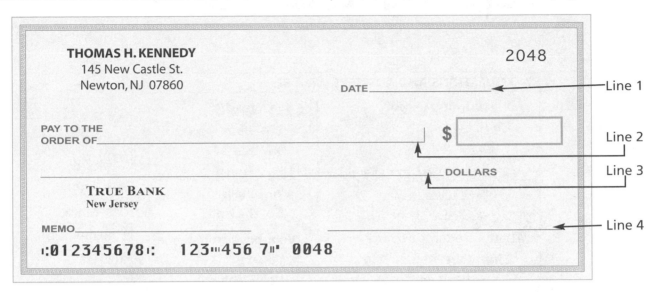

8. Thomas Kennedy writes a check to Newtown Drugs for $24.50 on 9/17/04. What is on Line 3?

   A. 9/17/04

   B. Newtown Drugs; $24.50

   C. Twenty-four and 50/100

   D. Medicine; Thomas Kennedy

9. What is on Line 1?

   A. 9/17/04

   B. Newtown Drugs; $24.50

   C. Twenty-four and 50/100

   D. Medicine; Thomas Kennedy

10. What is on Line 2?

   A. 9/17/04

   B. Newtown Drugs; $24.50

   C. Twenty-four and 50/100

   D. Medicine; Thomas Kennedy

HOW DID YOU DO? Count the number of correct answers on your answer sheet. Record this number in the bar graph on the inside back cover.

Spotlight: Grammar

YES/NO QUESTIONS AND ANSWERS WITH BE

Am I on State Street?
   Yes, **you are**.
   No, **you aren't**.

Are you from Mexico?
   Yes, **I am**.
   No, **I'm not**.

Are you and Tina from Canada?
   Yes, **we are**.
   No, **we aren't**.

Are the students in class?
   Yes, **they are**.
   No, **they aren't**.

Is Bob a teacher?
   Yes, **he is**.
   No, **he isn't**.

Is Tina a student?
   Yes, **she is**.
   No, **she isn't**.

Is your book from China?
   Yes, **it is**.
   No, **it isn't**.

People also say:
You're not.
He's not.
She's not.
We're not.
They're not.
It's not.

A Match the questions and answers.

Questions

1. Are you from the United States?
2. Is Fernando a student?
3. Is your school on State Street?
4. Are the teachers here?
5. Am I in your class?
6. Are you and Eugene at the bank?

Answers

a. Yes, we are.
b. No, you aren't.
c. Yes, he is.
d. No, it isn't.
e. No, they aren't.
f. Yes, I am.

B Read the story. Answer the questions.

Charles and Bernadette are in Mr. Harding's class. Charles is from the Ivory Coast. Bernadette is from the Ivory Coast, too. Bernadette is a nurse. Charles is a salesclerk. They are married.

1. Is Bernadette from Vietnam? _____
2. Are Bernadette and Charles students? _____
3. Are they in Mrs. Martin's class? _____
4. Are they single? _____

C Complete the chart.

Student	Country	Occupation	Marital status
Charles			
Bernadette			

46

INFORMATION QUESTIONS WITH *BE*						Contractions
What		your name?	What		your hours?	What's
Where		the supermarket?	Where		your books?	Where's
When	is	the next holiday?	When	are	banks open?	When's
Who		your teacher?	Who		Mutt and Jeff?	Who's
How much		one notebook?	How much		the notebooks?	

D Check the correct answer.

1. What is it?
   ☐ It's 3:30.   ☐ It's a book.

2. Who is your teacher?
   ☐ Tracy Edwards   ☐ in the classroom

3. How much is the book?
   ☐ It's on the desk.   ☐ It's $10.95.

4. Where are the pencils?
   ☐ They're on my desk.   ☐ Their last name is Lee.

5. When is the library open?
   ☐ on Bank Street   ☐ from 9:00 A.M. to 4:00 P.M.

E Write questions.

A: _____?
B: Terry Winter.

A: _____?
B: It's on Main Street.

A: _____?
B: 3215 Park Street.

A: _____?
B: They're from Russia.

When is your birthday?

A Write the missing months.

1. January	2. _____	3. _____	4. April
5. _____	6. June	7. _____	8. _____
9. _____	10. _____	11. November	12. _____

B Write the names of 2 months under each word.

EXAMPLE: *It's <u>hot</u> in <u>July</u>. It's <u>rainy</u> in <u>April</u>.*

Hot	Cold	Rainy	Sunny
July		*April*	
_____	_____	_____	_____
_____	_____	_____	_____

C Look at the graph. Write the number of birthdays for each month.

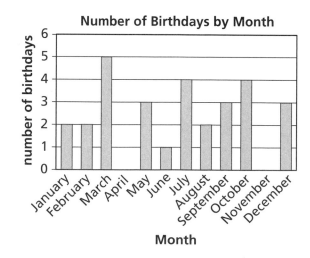

1. February _____2_____
2. March _____
3. April _____
4. July _____
5. November _____
6. December _____

D Circle the correct answer.

1. How many days are in a week?

   Ⓐ seven   B. four   c. twenty-four

2. How many days are in the month of July?

   A. twenty-four   B. twenty-eight   c. thirty-one

3. How many days are in the month of April?

   A. seven   B. thirty   c. twenty-eight

4. How many hours are in a day?

   A. thirty   B. twenty-eight   c. twenty-four

5. How many months are in a year?

   A. 24   B. 12   c. 7

6. How many minutes are in an hour?

   A. 30   B. 60   c. 100

How many ?

E Complete the survey.

ANSON COUNTY ADULT SCHOOL SURVEY

Please answer the questions below.

1. How many students are in your class?   _____

2. How many classes are in a week?   _____

3. What time is the class?   _____

4. What is your teacher's name?   _____

Circle the days of the class.

Mon.   Tues.   Wed.   Thurs.   Fri.   Sat.   Sun.

Circle the months of the class.

January   February   March   April   May   June   July   August   September   October   November   December

---

The party is on Sunday.

A Write the words next to the pictures.

doctor's appointment	PTO meeting	job interview
dentist's appointment	basketball game	birthday party

1. _____

2. _____

3. _____

4. _____

5. _____

6. _____

B Write the ordinal numbers.

EXAMPLE: ten → ___*tenth*___

1. one → _____
2. seven → _____
3. fifteen → _____
4. three → _____
5. nine → _____

6. 8 → _____
7. 13 → _____
8. 2 → _____
9. 5 → _____
10. 12 → _____

C Put the conversation in order. Number the sentences from first (1) to last (5).

_____ What day is that?

_____ Oh, sorry. I have a job interview on Thursday.

_____ It's Thursday.

__1__ Do you want to meet on the 2nd?

_____ Some other time, then.

D Look at the calendar. Match the questions and answers.

SUN.	MON.	TUES.	WED.	THURS.	FRI.	SAT.
	1	2 7:30 PTO meeting	3	4	5 8:00 P.M. basketball game	6 2:00 birthday party
7	8 9:00 A.M. job interview	9	10 1:30 P.M. dentist	11	12 3:30 P.M. Dr. Ling	13

Questions

1. When is your job interview?
2. What day is my dentist's appointment?
3. What date is the birthday party?
4. What time is the PTO meeting?
5. What day is your appointment with Dr. Ling?
6. What time is the basketball game?

Answers

a. It's at 7:30.
b. It's at 9:00 A.M. on the 8th.
c. It's the 6th.
d. It's on Friday.
e. It's Wednesday, the 10th.
f. It's at 8:00 P.M.

E Answer the questions about you.

1. Do you have a job interview? When? _____

2. When is your next birthday? _____

3. What appointments are on your calendar? _____

3
LESSON

What's the date?

A Write the numbers another way.

EXAMPLE: _____4th_____ = fourth

1. _____ = seventeenth

2. 22nd = _____

3. 20th = _____

4. _____ = twenty-third

5. 28th = _____

B Look at the card. Answer the questions.

Sarah Parker

HAS A DENTIST'S
APPOINTMENT ON:

May 13 **at** 2:30 p.m.

☐ MON. ☐ TUES. ☐ WED. ☑ THURS. ☐ FRI.

1. What day is the appointment?

   _____

2. What time is it? _____

3. Who is the appointment for?

   _____

4. What date is it?

   _____

C Circle the correct answer.

EXAMPLE: My appointment is on the _____.

   Ⓐ 8th   B. 2

1. There are _____ students in my class.

   A. 25   B. 25th

2. I have a meeting on the _____.

   A. five   B. fifth

3. There is a game on the _____ of March.

   A. 21st   B. 12

4. My birthday is the _____ of February.

   A. one   B. first

5. December is the _____ month.

   A. twelfth   B. 12

6. There are _____ Mondays in July.

   A. 22nd   B. four

D Write the dates another way.

1. 2/9/05 = _____
2. 7/15/99 = _____
3. August 1, 2002 = _____
4. 5/31/1960 = _____
5. March 3, 1991 = _____

6. 01/01/03 = _____
7. April 9, 2001 = _____
8. 12/25/72 = _____
9. 9/12/06 = _____
10. June 8, 1995 = _____

E Write the words in the correct order. Write questions and answers.

EXAMPLE: What/doctor's appointment/is/your/time
    What time is your doctor's appointment?

1. A: the basketball game/is/What day

    _____?

   B: on Friday/It's

    _____.

2. A: the PTO meeting/is/When

    _____?

   B: It's/13th/March/on

    _____.

3. A: is that/day/What

    _____?

   B: Tuesday/It's

    _____.

F Write the information on the card.

Day of the week: Monday   Name: Michiko Jones
Date: 12/8/04   Time: 10:30 A.M.

_____

has a dentist's appointment on:

_____ at _____

M T W TH F

4 LESSON

Holidays

A Complete the sentences.

ACROSS

1. The holiday on February 14th is _____ Day.

3. July 4th is _____ Day.

4. _____ is on the fourth Thursday in November.

6. The first day of January is _____ Day.

DOWN

2. _____ is the first Tuesday after the first Monday in November.

5. Labor _____ is on the first Monday in September.

B Write the words in the crossword puzzle below.

C Write the holidays in order.

New Year's Day	Labor Day	Election Day
Valentine's Day	Thanksgiving	Independence Day

1. First: _____ *New Year's Day* _____

2. Second: _____

3. Third: _____

4. Fourth: _____

5. Fifth: _____

6. Sixth: _____

D Write the words in the correct place in the chart.

| desks | students | book | hour | city |
| teacher | holidays | words | week | libraries |

SINGULAR	PLURAL
book	desks

E Write the plural forms.

EXAMPLE: pen _____pens_____

1. drugstore _____
2. day _____
3. stoplight _____
4. penny _____
5. restaurant _____

6. minute _____
7. notebook _____
8. telephone _____
9. dollar _____
10. family _____

F Answer the questions with numbers and words.

EXAMPLE: How many days are in a week? _____seven days_____

1. How many classrooms are in your school? _____
2. How many teachers are in your class? _____
3. How many books are on your desk? _____
4. How many holidays are in this month? _____
5. How many libraries are near your school? _____

G Read the story. Write about your classroom.

My name is ___Karen___. I am in my classroom. There are _22 students_ in my class. Mr. _Robert_ is the teacher. Our class is ___four days___ a week, from Monday to Thursday. Our class is _three hours_ long, _from 6:00 P.M. to 9:00 P.M._ .

_____

_____

_____

What events are on Saturday?

A Read the newspaper below. Circle the times and days.

July 2, 2005

MIAMI NEWS

WEEKEND EVENTS

TODAY	SATURDAY	SUNDAY
MOVIES **In the Park** **7:00 P.M. "Star Battles"** In Marshall Park, Forest Street. Free. **INTERNATIONAL FESTIVAL, Elm and Long Streets, 8:00-10:00 P.M.** There are more than 20 restaurants (from many countries: Mexico, China, Japan, France, Colombia) at the festival. Great food! $3 admission.	**COMMUNITY FUN DAY** **Alden Community Center,** **1:00-3:00 P.M.** Look at the new school. Many classes for adults and children. Talk to the teachers, see the classrooms, play games. 3215 Caldwell Street. Information call: (305) 555-9044. **LIBRARY BIRTHDAY PARTY Main Library, 4:00 P.M.** The Centerville Library is 100 years old. A 100th birthday party for children in grades K-8. Librarians and writers read books out loud. For information, call (305) 555-8873.	**INDEPENDENCE DAY** **PARADE, Main Street,** **begins 5:00 P.M. Fireworks** **at 9:00 P.M. in Central Park.** The big party starts at 5:00 with the parade. See the fireworks at 9:00 P.M. Bring the children. 

B Match the events and places.

Events	Places
1. Independence Day fireworks	a. Marshall Park
2. Library Birthday Party	b. Elm and Long Streets
3. Movie	c. 3215 Caldwell Street
4. Community Center Fun Day	d. Central Park
5. International Festival	e. Main Library

56

C Answer the questions.

1. What events are on Saturday?

_____ and _____

2. What events are for children?

_____, _____ and _____

3. What events are parties?

_____ and _____

D Complete the sentences. Use information from the newspaper.

1. The International Festival is from _____ to _____ P.M.

2. The festival has food from these countries: _____, _____, _____,

_____ and _____.

3. It is $_____ to go to the festival.

4. The address of the Alden Community Center is _____.

5. The Community Fun Day at the community center is on _____, from _____ to

_____ P.M.

6. Sunday is a holiday. It is _____ Day.

7. The date for Sunday is _____.

8. There is a movie in _____ Park on Friday.

9. The library is _____ years old. There is a _____ party at the library.

10. The party is for children in grades _____.

★ ★

TAKE IT OUTSIDE: Find a newspaper for your city or town. Read about events. Write 2 events for this week or month in your town.

EVENT	DATE	TIME	PLACE
basketball game	1/19/04	8 P.M.	City Arena

★ ★

Here's my schedule.

A Read the story. Answer the questions.

Isabel Lee is a painter. In her job, she paints houses and other buildings. This month her job is at the Alden Community Center. There are 6 new classrooms at the community center. Isabel paints the new classrooms. She paints 1 classroom in 2 days. The first day for students in the new classrooms is Monday, June 28. Isabel paints on Monday to Friday, not on Saturday and Sunday. She writes her schedule on a calendar.

1. What is Isabel's last name?   _____ *Lee* _____

2. Where is her job this month?   _____

3. How many new classrooms are there?   _____

4. How many days is it to paint 1 classroom? _____

5. What days does Isabel paint?   _____

6. When is the first day for students?   _____

B Look at Isabel's schedule for June.

Sunday	Monday	Tuesday	Wednesday	Thursday	Friday	Saturday
		1	2	3	4	5
6	7	8	9	10 Start room 1	11 Finish room 1	12
13	14	15	16	17	18	19
20	21	22	23	24	25 Finish room 6	26
27	28 First day of classes	29	30			

Write the dates Isabel paints the rooms.

	Start	Finish
Room 1	6/10	6/11
Room 2	_____	_____
Room 3	_____	_____
Room 4	_____	_____
Room 5	_____	_____
Room 6	_____	6/25

C Write the information on the calendar above.

EXAMPLE:

10 Start room 1	11 Finish room 1

★ ★

TAKE IT OUTSIDE: Interview a family member, friend, or coworker. Write 3 things that person has to do at work this week on the calendar below.

SUNDAY	MONDAY	TUESDAY	WEDNESDAY	THURSDAY	FRIDAY	SATURDAY

★ ★

Practice Test

DIRECTIONS: Answer the questions. Use the Answer Sheet.

1. Your appointment is on Friday.

A.
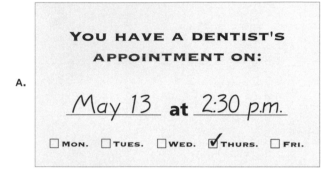

B.

C.
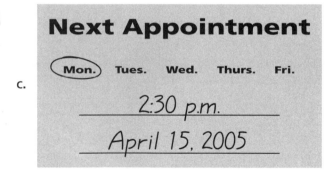

D.
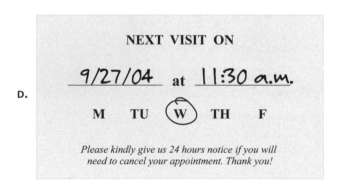

2. It's on Tuesday.

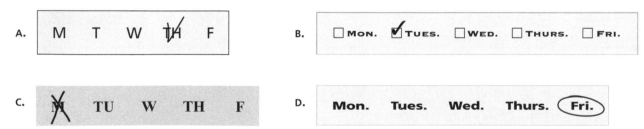

3. It's January twenty-fifth.

   A. 25/01/06   B. 2/25/06

   C. 1/25/06   D. 01/06/25

4. His birth date is 04/12/62.

   A. December 4, 1962   B. April 12, 2004

   C. April 12, 1962   D. December 12, 2004

ANSWER SHEET								
1. Ⓐ Ⓑ Ⓒ Ⓓ				6. Ⓐ Ⓑ Ⓒ Ⓓ				
2. Ⓐ Ⓑ Ⓒ Ⓓ				7. Ⓐ Ⓑ Ⓒ Ⓓ				
3. Ⓐ Ⓑ Ⓒ Ⓓ				8. Ⓐ Ⓑ Ⓒ Ⓓ				
4. Ⓐ Ⓑ Ⓒ Ⓓ				9. Ⓐ Ⓑ Ⓒ Ⓓ				
5. Ⓐ Ⓑ Ⓒ Ⓓ				10. Ⓐ Ⓑ Ⓒ Ⓓ				

5. What month is it?

    A. Wednesday   B. August

    C. 1978   D. 6:15 P.M.

DIRECTIONS: Look at the calendar to answer the next 5 questions. Use the Answer Sheet on page 60.

JULY						
SUN.	MON.	TUES.	WED.	THURS.	FRI.	SAT.
		1	2	3	4	5
6	7	8	9	10	11	12
13	14	15	16	17	18	19
20	21	22	23	24	25	26
27	28	29	30	31		

6. July begins on what day of the week?

    A. Monday   B. Tuesday

    C. Wednesday   D. Thursday

7. What day of the week is July 31st?

    A. Monday   B. Tuesday

    C. Wednesday   D. Thursday

8. You have a dentist appointment on July 15. What day is it?

    A. Monday   B. Tuesday

    C. Wednesday   D. Thursday

9. Sandy has a job interview on the 23rd. What day is it?

    A. Monday   B. Tuesday

    C. Wednesday D. Thursday

10. It is the second Friday in July. What is the date?

    A. 7/3/03   B. 7/2/03

    C. 7/11/03   D. 11/7/03

HOW DID YOU DO? Count the number of correct answers on your answer sheet. Record this number in the bar graph on the inside back cover.

Shirts, Skirts, and Sweaters

A Write the words in the correct place in the chart.

necktie	shirt	socks
undershirt	sweater	pants
briefs	hat	shorts
shoes	T-shirt	blouse
boots	jacket	skirt
coat	pajamas	dress

SINGULAR	PLURAL
necktie	*socks*

B Complete the sentences. Write *is* or *are*.

1. What color _is_ the necktie?
2. What color _____ the socks?
3. My boots _____ brown.
4. Susan's sweater _____ blue.
5. Where _____ my shoes?
6. There _____ a coat on the table.
7. Tony's pajamas _____ gray.
8. My socks _____ in the car.
9. Her skirt _____ yellow.
10. Where _____ his black pants?
11. Where _____ my white T-shirt?

> *is* for singular/*are* for plural

C Complete the sentences. Write *is*, *am*, or *are*.

1. A: What _____ John wearing?

   B: He _____ wearing a blue sweater.

is	am	are

2. A: Where _____ my green dress?

   B: I _____ wearing it.

3. A: I _____ wearing a red blouse.

   B: No, you _____ not. Your blouse _____ pink.

4. A: _____ Lana wearing a dress?

   B: No, she _____ not. She _____ wearing a skirt.

5. A: What _____ Sara and Tom wearing?

   B: They _____ wearing orange shirts.

D Look at the picture. Check *yes* or *no*.

	YES	NO
1. Sonia is wearing a hat.		✓
2. Michael is wearing shorts.		
3. Gordon is wearing a T-shirt.		
4. Michael is wearing a necktie.		
5. Gordon is wearing pants.		
6. Sonia is wearing boots.		

E Read the story. Write about you.

Charlie's favorite color is red. Today he is wearing a blue shirt and black pants. His shoes are brown.

My favorite color is _____

_____

_____

_____

_____

I'm looking for children's clothes.

A Find these words in the puzzle. Circle them.

necktie	socks	undershirt	sweater	pants
shorts	shoes	T-shirt ✓	pajamas	skirt
exit	cashier	boots	jacket	coat

```
W  S  W  L  F (T  S  H  I  R  T) C
P  H  J  A  C  K  E  T  C  S  E  A
A  O  B  O  O  T  S  O  C  K  S  S
N  E  C  K  T  I  E  D  O  I  E  H
T  S  W  E  A  T  E  R  A  R  X  I
S  H  O  R  T  S  Y  E  T  T  I  E
O  P  A  J  A  M  A  S  U  L  T  R
Z  U  N  D  E  R  S  H  I  R  T  J
```

B Put the conversation in order. Number the sentences from first (1) to last (6).

_____ The third floor?

_1_ Can I help you?

_____ They're on the third floor.

_____ That's right.

_____ Yes, I'm looking for children's clothes.

_____ Thanks.

C Circle the correct answer.

1. Where's Claudio?

   (A.) He's near the entrance.   B. Yes, thank you.

2. Where are Martin and Song?

   A. They're on the first floor.   B. That's right.

3. What's she doing?

   A. On the first floor.   B. She's sleeping.

64

4. Where are women's coats?

   A. On the first floor.   B. Can I help you?

5. Where is the fitting room?

   A. It's near the exit.   B. She's near the exit.

6. What are Ron and Diana doing?

   A. We're going into the fitting room.   B. They're leaving.

D Complete the sentences. Write *is, am,* or *are.*

1. I _____*am*_____ going to school.

2. We _____ going into the department store.

3. They _____ talking to the teacher.

4. Annette _____ sitting in the classroom.

5. You _____ leaving with Sam.

6. He _____ sleeping.

> **is/am/are + actions (-ing)**

E Write about you. Use words from the box to complete the chart.

the classroom	pants	the library	socks
the supermarket	shoes	the park	a shirt
a coat	my job	a skirt	a dress
school	a necktie		

I AM GOING TO:	I AM WEARING:
school	a necktie

What size is it?

A Write the words in order of size: *extra large, medium, small, large.*

_____small_____ < _____ < _____ < _____

B Write the words next to the letters.

S ——————————————   L ——————————————

M ——————————————   XL ——————————————

C Circle the correct answer.

1. That's a nice shirt. What size is it?

   A. blue   (B.) medium   C. $12.50

2. Is it on sale?

   A. Yes, it's 50 percent off.   B. It's a small.   C. It's near the exit.

3. What size is the jacket?

   A. It's a large.   B. It's black.   C. It's a good price.

4. What color are the shoes?

   A. They're large.   B. They're on sale.   C. They're brown.

5. How much is it?

   A. $5.00   B. It's on sale.   C. That's a good price.

6. That's a nice dress. How much is it?

   A. It's a large.   B. It's $25.00.   C. It's near the exit.

D Write the symbols.

	Symbols	
times (x)	divided by (÷)	equals (=)
3 x 2 = 6	6 ÷ 2 = 3	

1. 5 __x__ 3 __=__ 15.

2. 6 _____ 3 _____ 18.

3. 20 _____ 5 _____ 4

4. 2 _____ 4 _____ 8.

5. 30 _____ 3 _____ 10

6. 24 _____ 8 _____ 3

E Look at the clothes. Write the amounts of money.

$10

1 blouse = $10.00

3 x $10 =

$30

$2

1 pair of socks = _____

2 x _____ =

$20.00

$20

1 pair of shoes =

$12

1 necktie = _____

___ x _____ =

$15

1 pair of pants =

$15.00

How much money is it for all the clothes? TOTAL =

F Write about you.

1. I wear a size _____ T-shirt.

2. My jacket is a size _____.

3. My favorite color for pants is _____.

4. _____ is a good price for shoes.

5. The name of my department store is _____.

LESSON 4

A Folktale

A Learn new words. Find and circle these words in the story.

wash/washes	dirty	soap
mud	food stains	line dry

1. This is a story about a boy named Hans.

> Hans, please go to the store and buy some soap. Say "soap, soap, soap" so you don't forget.

> Okay, mama. Soap, soap, soap...

2. Hans walks down the street. He walks into a hole with mud in it and gets dirty.

> Oh no. What is it? I forget.

> What are you looking for? This street is slippery like soap.

> Soap. Soap. Soap. Soap.

> Don't repeat what I say. Say you're sorry.

3. Hans walks down the street. He walks into a woman with eggs and milk.

> I'm sorry. I'm sorry. I'm sorry.

> I know you're sorry. Can't you see I need help!

4. Hans helps the woman stand up. He walks down the street. He sees a blind man.

> Can't you see! I need help! Can't you see! I need help!

> I can't see. But I can smell. You are dirty and need to wash!

5. Hans goes into the store. He is very dirty. There is mud on his pants. There are food stains on his shirt.

> I am dirty and need to wash! I am dirty and need to wash!

> You need some soap.

> I need some soap! I need some soap!

6. Hans is happy. He buys the soap. He goes home and washes. His mother washes his shirt and his pants. She hangs them up to line dry.

B Put the sentences in order. Number the events from first (1) to last (10).

_____ Hans buys soap at the store.

_____ Hans bumps into an old woman.

_____ Hans's mother washes his dirty clothes.

_____ Hans steps in a hole.

_____ Hans helps the woman. She stands up.

___1___ Hans's mother asks Hans to go to the store.

_____ Hans sees an old man.

_____ A man tells Hans the street is slippery.

_____ An old man tells Hans to wash.

_____ Hans goes into the store.

C Rewrite the sentences in Activity B. Use object pronouns.

EXAMPLE: Hans buys soap at the store.

Hans buys it at the store.

object pronouns: *me, you, her, him, it, them, us*

1. _____

2. _____

3. _____

4. _____

5. _____

6. _____

7. _____

8. _____

9. _____

10. _____

D Look at the labels for Hans's shirt and pants. Answer the questions.

Hans's Pants

40C ▢ △
WASH HOT WATER
LINE DRY ONLY
NO BLEACH

M

Hans's Shirt

▢
HAND WASH
COLD WATER
LINE DRY

SMALL

1. What temperature should you wash the shirt in?

☐ cold   ☐ warm

2. What temperature should you wash the pants in?

☐ cold   ☐ hot

3. Should you line dry the pants?

☐ yes   ☐ no

4. What size is the shirt?

☐ small   ☐ medium

COMMUNITY LESSON

I'd like a refund.

A Read the story. Answer the questions.

Karina is a student. She is wearing some blue pants. The pants are too big. She'd like to return the pants. Casual Clothes is the store. Karina doesn't live near the store. Casual Clothes sends the clothes in the mail. Karina sends the pants back to Casual Clothes in the mail. She sends a form with the pants. She says the pants are too big.

1. What is the student's name? _____

2. What is the name of the store? _____

3. What color are the pants? _____

4. What's the problem? _____

5. Is the store near Karina? _____

B Learn new words. Find and circle these words on the form.

exchange	refund	gift certificate

Step 1
Fill out Customer Information.
Customer Information:
Name: _Karina Stark_
Address: _7325 Meadow Street_
City: _Madison_   State: _WI_
Daytime phone: _(608) 555-5433_

Step 2
How would you like us to handle your return?
☐ Exchange item
☑ Refund
☐ Gift certificate

Step 3
List the item(s) you are returning. Include the reason. (See chart below.)

Reason	Description	Color	Price
21	Pants	Blue	$25.00

Problem:
11 – too small   12 – too short
21 – too big   22 – too long
31 – don't like color
41 – don't like style

C Look at the form. Check the information you see.

☑ name of customer

☐ address of customer

☐ problem with clothes

☐ telephone number of customer

☐ description of clothes

☐ color of clothes

☐ size of clothes

☐ city

☐ school

☐ price

☐ how to handle the return

D Your brown coat is too small. It is $50.00. Complete the form.

Step 1	Step 3
Fill out Customer Information. **Customer Information:** Name: _____ Address: _____ City: _____ State: ____ Daytime phone: _____	List the item(s) you are returning. Include the reason. (See chart below.)

Step 3
List the item(s) you are returning. Include the reason.
(See chart below.)

Reason	Description	Color	Price

Problem:

11 – too small	12 – too short
21 – too big	22 – too long
31 – don't like color	
41 – don't like style	

Step 2
How would you like us to handle your return?
☐ Exchange item
☐ Refund
☐ Gift certificate

★ ★

TAKE IT OUTSIDE: Go to a store. Look for a sign: "Return Policy." Write down the words. Bring them to class. Talk about them with your teacher and classmates.

★ ★

His pants are too large.

North Park School Uniform

Approved Clothing Articles

Shirts: White

Pants, Slacks, Shorts: Blue

Skirts: Blue

Necktie: Any color

Sweaters: White or blue

Accessories:

Socks or tights should be blue or white.

Do NOT wear to school:

T-Shirts, pants that are too large, shorts that are too short, clothes that are too tight, shirts cut too low, blue jeans

The following is a list of stores that carry school uniforms or clothing that meets the uniform guidelines:

Barton's Department Store, BigMart, Clothes for Kids (in store & mail order)

A Circle *yes* or *no* for the sentences about North Park School.

1. Students can wear shorts.	(yes)	no
2. Students can wear jeans.	yes	no
3. Shirts are blue or white.	yes	no
4. Socks are black or white.	yes	no
5. Students can wear T-shirts.	yes	no
6. Pants can be too large.	yes	no

B Write the words in the correct place.

Blue clothes
pants

Blue or white

White clothes

C Match the clothes and problems.

Clothes	Problems
1. shorts	a. too tight
2. pants	b. too short
3. shirts	c. too large
4. clothes	d. cut too low

D Complete the sentences.

1. Mrs. Long: What's the problem?

   Teacher: Sarah's shorts are too _____.

2. Mrs. Harris: Michael's pants are not good for school. He needs a small.

   Mr. Harris: Are his pants too _____?

3. Teacher: There is a problem. David is wearing a _____.

   Mr. Tang: I'm sorry.

★ ★

TAKE IT OUTSIDE: Interview a family member, friend, or coworker. Ask the questions. Write the answers.

1. Does your child wear a uniform? _____

2. What clothes can he or she wear to school? _____

   _____

3. What clothes are <u>not</u> for school? _____

★ ★

REVIEW

LESSON

Practice Test

DIRECTIONS: Answer the questions. Use the Answer Sheet.

1. Susan wears a large.

   A. L

   B. M

   C. S

   D. XL

2. What size is it?

   A. blue

   B. medium

   C. $7.99

   D. too loose

3. How much is it?

   A. blue

   B. medium

   C. $7.99

   D. too loose

	ANSWER SHEET			
1	A	B	C	D
2	A	B	C	D
3	A	B	C	D
4	A	B	C	D
5	A	B	C	D
6	A	B	C	D
7	A	B	C	D
8	A	B	C	D
9	A	B	C	D
10	A	B	C	D

DIRECTIONS: Look at the price tag to answer the next 3 questions. Use the Answer Sheet.

XL

Men's shirt/green

**Regular price:
$20.00**

Sale price

$12.99

4. What size is it?

   A. small

   B. medium

   C. large

   D. extra large

5. What is the price on sale?

   A. $20.00

   B. 50% off

   C. $12.99

   D. $7.01

6. How much less is the sale price than the regular price?

   A. $20.00   B. 50% off

   C. $12.99   D. $7.01

DIRECTIONS: Look at the shirt label to answer the next 2 questions. Use the Answer Sheet on page 74.

MACHINE WASH
COLD

DO NOT BLEACH

LINE DRY

WARM IRON

MADE IN CHINA

100% COTTON

L

7. What size is the shirt?

   A. cotton

   B. cold

   C. dry

   D. large

8. What water temperature should you use to wash the shirt?

   A. cold

   B. cool

   C. warm

   D. hot

DIRECTIONS: Answer the questions. Use the Answer Sheet on page 74.

9. Lilian wears <u>red socks</u> on Mondays. Which object pronoun is correct?

   A. her

   B. it

   C. them

   D. us

10. I like <u>Mrs. Adams</u>. Which object pronoun is correct?

    A. her

    B. him

    C. them

    D. it

HOW DID YOU DO? Count the number of correct answers on your answer sheet. Record this number in the bar graph on the inside back cover.

Spotlight: Grammar

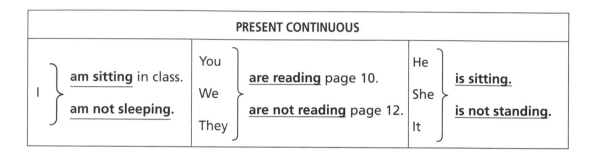

PRESENT CONTINUOUS

I { **am sitting** in class. / **am not sleeping.**

You / We / They { **are reading** page 10. / **are not reading** page 12.

He / She / It { **is sitting.** / **is not standing.**

A Complete the sentences. Write *am, is, are, am not, isn't,* or *aren't.*

1. Maria __is__ sitting. She isn't standing.

2. We _____ going to the store. We are watching TV.

3. Greg and Nancy are in class. They _____ learning English.

4. I'm not home. I _____ buying clothes at the department store.

5. The sales clerk is reading a book. She _____ helping customers.

6. You are talking. You _____ listening to the teacher.

B Rewrite the sentences. Use the present continuous.

1. On Mondays, I go to the store.
   _____ *I am going to the store now.* _____

2. On Tuesdays, I study English.
   _____

3. Every day she reads her book.
   _____

4. On Fridays, the library opens at 10:00 A.M.
   _____

5. In the afternoon, we listen to the radio.
   _____

6. In the morning, they sleep.
   _____

INFORMATION QUESTIONS WITH THE PRESENT CONTINUOUS					
What		she reading?	What		you reading?
Where	**is**	he sitting?	Where	**are**	they sitting?
Why		Mr. Smith leaving?	Why		Mr. and Mrs. Smith leaving?
Who		sitting down?	Who		you talking to?

C Check the correct answer.

1. Why are they going home?
   - ☐ at 3:00 P.M.
   - ☑ Their class is over.

2. Who is living there?
   - ☐ Mr. and Mrs. Zinberg
   - ☐ 1329 South Street

3. What are you buying?
   - ☐ BigMart
   - ☐ a black sweater

4. Where are you sitting?
   - ☐ next to Darren
   - ☐ I'm listening to the teacher.

D Write the words in the correct order. Then answer the questions.

1. _____?   is/standing/by the board/Who

2. _____?   you/wearing/are/What/today

3. _____?   Where/your parents/living/are

4. _____?   learning/you/Why/are/English

5. _____?   is/in the class/Who/listening

Noodles are delicious.

A Write the words in the correct place in the chart. (More than 1 idea is possible.)

oranges	bananas	butter	beans
grapes	apples	lettuce	carrots

YELLOW	GREEN	ORANGE
	beans	

B Complete the sentences. Write *is* or *are*.

1. Bananas _____*are*_____ good.
2. Carrots _____ orange.
3. Milk _____ white.
4. I think rice _____ delicious.
5. There _____ onions on the table.
6. _____ there some butter on the table?
7. Where _____ the tomatoes?
8. There _____ cheese on the bread.

is/are

C Look at Henry's food for this week. Answer the questions.

SUN.	MON.	TUES.	WED.	THURS.	FRI.	SAT.
rice and shrimp	chicken	shrimp and tomatoes	noodles	rice and beans	bread and cheese	chicken and carrots

1. What food is for Monday? _____*chicken*_____
2. What food is for Wednesday? _____
3. Does Henry have rice on Sunday? _____
4. What day does Henry have carrots? _____
5. When does he have beans? _____
6. What day does he eat tomatoes? _____

D Make a schedule of your food. Write one food for each day.

SUN.	MON.	TUES.	WED.	THURS.	FRI.	SAT.

E Read the story. Check *yes* or *no*.

Henry likes rice. He thinks rice is delicious. Henry doesn't like onions. He thinks onions are terrible. Henry thinks oranges and grapes are good. He doesn't think that yogurt is good.

1. Henry likes yogurt.   ☐ yes ☐ no
2. He doesn't like rice.   ☐ yes ☐ no
3. Henry likes grapes.   ☐ yes ☐ no
4. He doesn't like onions.   ☐ yes ☐ no
5. He likes oranges.   ☐ yes ☐ no

F Answer the questions about you. Write *Yes, I do*, or *No, I don't*.

1. Do you like peanuts? _____

2. Do you like bananas? _____

3. Do you like rice? _____

4. Do you think apples are delicious? _____

5. Do you think onions are terrible? _____

6. Do you think carrots are good? _____

questions and answers
with *do* and *don't*

G Write about you. Use sentences from Activities E and F.

_____

_____

_____

_____

_____

2 LESSON

Do you sell rice?

A Make words from the letters.

bakery	restroom	produce section	canned goods
✓ fruit	vegetables	frozen food	dairy

1. u t i f r _____ *fruit* _____

2. k a r y b e _____

3. f n z o o e d o r f _____

4. g l e s a v e b e t _____

5. o d c a o d d n s e n g _____

6. i d y a r _____

B Complete the sentences. Use words from box above.

1. Bread is in the _____ section.

2. _____ and _____ are in the produce section.

3. There is milk and cheese in the _____ section.

C Circle the correct answer.

1. Excuse me. Do you sell cereal?

   A. You're welcome.   Ⓑ Yes, we do.

2. It's in Aisle 1.

   A. Aisle 1?   B. Excuse me.

3. Thanks a lot.

   A. No, we don't.   B. You're welcome.

4. Excuse me. Do you sell peanuts?

   A. No, we don't.   B. Thanks a lot.

5. Do you sell oranges?

   A. It's in the produce section.   B. They're in the produce section.

6. Do you sell butter?

   A. It's in the dairy section.   B. They're in the dairy section.

80

D Look at the photos. Write the letter next to the sentence.

A   B   C

1. She is in the produce section.   _____

2. She is looking at the canned goods.   _____

3. He is at the checkout counter.   _____

E Check *yes* or *no* about the photos.

1. In photo A, the woman is wearing a jacket.   ☑ yes   ☐ no

2. In photo B, they are near the fruit.   ☐ yes   ☐ no

3. In photo C, the man is cleaning the floor.   ☐ yes   ☐ no

4. In photo B, the salesclerk has a banana.   ☐ yes   ☐ no

5. There are some oranges in photo A.   ☐ yes   ☐ no

6. The customer in photo B is pushing a cart.   ☐ yes   ☐ no

3

LESSON

How much is it?

A Match the foods and containers. (More than 1 answer is possible.)

Foods	Containers
1. ____h____ bread	a. jar
2. _____ sugar	b. package
3. _____ milk	c. bag
4. _____ apples	d. bottle
5. _____ cheese	e. box
6. _____ honey	f. carton
7. _____ tomatoes	g. can
8. _____ cereal	h. loaf
9. _____ rice	
10. _____ oil	

B Write the name of the container under the picture. Then write 2 foods for each container.

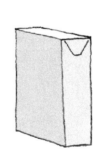

_____

1. _____oil_____

2. _____

_____

1. _____

2. _____

_____

1. _____

2. _____

_____

1. _____

2. _____

C Write the amounts another way.

1. 2 cups = _____32 tablespoons_____ (tbsp.)

2. 2 lbs = _____ (oz.)

3. 2 cups = _____ (oz.)

4. 24 ounces = _____ (lbs.)

5. $\frac{1}{2}$ cup = _____ (oz.)

6. 12 fluid ounces = _____ (cup)

> 1 pound (lb) = 16 ounces (oz.)
>
> 1 cup = 8 fluid ounces (oz.)
>
> 16 tablespoons = 1 cup

D Look at the food labels. Answer the questions below.

FRESH SHRIMP

NET WT	UNIT PRICE	SOLD ON
2.0	$6.99/LB	06/08/04

TOTAL PRICE
$13.98

CHICKEN

NET WT	UNIT PRICE	SOLD ON
5.0	$3.00/LB	09/15/05

TOTAL PRICE
$15.00

CHEESE

NET WT	UNIT PRICE	SOLD ON
.5	$4.50/LB	01/10/03

TOTAL PRICE
$2.25

PEANUTS

NET WT	UNIT PRICE	SOLD ON
1.0	$6.99/LB	11/23/05

TOTAL PRICE
$6.99

1. How much money is 1 pound of shrimp?   _$6.99_

2. How much money is the package of shrimp?   _____

3. How many pounds is the package of chicken?   _____

4. How many pounds is the cheese?   _____

5. How much money are the peanuts?   _____

6. How much money is 1 pound of chicken?   _____

LESSON 4

Store Flyers

A Read the store flyer. Write the regular prices and the sale prices. Subtract to find the savings.

FOOD	REGULAR PRICE	SALE PRICE	SAVINGS
Milk	$3.00	(2/$5 =) $2.50	$.50

B Write the amounts.

1. What is the amount of milk? _____64 ounces_____

2. What is the amount of honey? _____

3. What is the amount of carrots? _____

C Match the questions and answers.

Questions	Answers	
		frequency adverbs

1. __c__ How often do you eat rice?

2. _____ How often do you eat shrimp?

3. _____ Do you have milk every day?

4. _____ Do you eat at restaurants?

5. _____ Do you eat cereal in the mornings?

6. _____ How often do you drink juice?

a. I always drink juice in the morning.

b. I rarely eat shrimp.

c. I always eat rice for dinner.

d. I often eat cereal in the mornings.

e. I sometimes eat at restaurants.

f. I never have milk.

D Write about you. Complete the sentences with *always, often, sometimes, rarely,* or *never.*

frequency adverbs

1. I _____ drink juice in the morning.

2. I _____ eat bananas.

3. I _____ go to the supermarket on Saturday.

4. I _____ look at the prices of food.

5. I _____ ask the salesclerk at the supermarket for help.

E Read the store receipt. Write the information.

```
       SAVEMOR'S
       SUPERMARKET


2 lb @ .50/lb
     bananas      $1.00

3 lb @ $2.00/lb
     chicken      $6.00

cereal            $4.99
     SALE        -$2.00
                  $2.99
```

1. Number of pounds of bananas: ___2___

2. Number of pounds of chicken: _____

3. Price of chicken per pound: _____

4. Regular price of cereal: _____

5. Sale price of cereal: _____

6. Savings on cereal: _____

85

COMMUNITY

LESSON

Jim always compares prices.

A Learn new words. Find and circle these words in the story.

shop/shops	buy/buys	low/lowest
cost/costs	compare/compares	high/highest

Jim is shopping for food today. Jim goes to the supermarket every Saturday. He usually shops in the morning. Jim buys food for his family. Sometimes he goes to Savemor's Supermarket and sometimes he goes to BigMart. He never goes to Fancy Foods. The prices at Savemor's and BigMart are often low. The food at Fancy Foods always costs more. Jim always compares prices. The prices at Fancy food are the highest.

B Complete the sentences. Use frequency adverbs.

1. _____*Sometimes*_____ he goes to Savemor's Supermarket.

2. He_____ shops in the morning.

3. _____ he goes to BigMart.

4. The food at Fancy Foods _____ costs more.

5. Jim _____ compares prices.

6. The prices at BigMart are _____ good.

> **frequency adverbs: always, usually, sometimes, never, often**

C Look at the chart. Circle the lowest price for each food.

Food	Fancy Foods	BigMart	Savemor's
Milk (64 oz.)	$3.59	$3.13	$2.99
Bananas (1 lb.)	$.89	$.59	$.65
Shrimp (1 lb.)	$12.99	$8.99	$5.99
Butter (1 lb.)	$3.75	$3.35	$3.50

D Look at the chart in Activity C. Circle the correct answer.

1. How much is one pound of bananas at Fancy Foods?

   Ⓐ $.89　　　　　B. $.59　　　　　C. $.65

2. How much is 1 pound of butter at Savemor's?

   A. $.65　　　　　B. $5.99　　　　　C. $3.50

3. Where is the highest price for milk?

   A. Fancy Foods　　　　B. BigMart　　　　C. Savemor's

4. Where will Jim spend the lowest amount on shrimp?

   A. Fancy Foods　　　　B. BigMart　　　　C. Savemor's

5. How much is 1 pound of shrimp at BigMart?

   A. $12.99　　　　　B. $8.99　　　　　C. $5.99

6. Jim buys bananas for $.65 at Savemor's. How much does he spend at Fancy Foods?

   A. $3.59　　　　　B. $.89　　　　　C. $12.99

high < higher < highest price
$$$$　$$$$$　$$$$$$
low > lower > lowest
$$$　$$　　$

★ ★

TAKE IT OUTSIDE: Go to 2 stores near your home. Write the prices in the chart.

FOOD	1ST STORE (WRITE NAME) _____	2ND STORE (WRITE NAME) _____
Bananas (1 lb.)		
Green grapes (1 lb.)		

★ ★

What can I get for you?

A Read the story. Complete the sentences. Use words from the story.

Deli Sandwiches

Arton works in a <u>deli</u> restaurant. Customers ask Arton for <u>sandwiches</u>. There are two pieces of bread in a sandwich. Often there is meat and cheese between the two pieces of bread. Sometimes, people ask for vegetables on the sandwich. Arton circles the type of meat, cheese, and vegetables on a sandwich form. Customers say what type of bread they want. Arton circles the bread, too. In some deli restaurants, the customers circle what they want.

1. _____A sandwich_____ often has _____ and _____ between two pieces of bread.

    Sometimes, there are _____ on the sandwich.

2. A _____deli_____ is a _____ or store. Customers ask for _____ at a deli.

B Answer the questions about Arton. Check *yes* or *no*.

1. Does Arton work in a supermarket?   ☐ yes   ☐ no

2. Does Arton make sandwiches?   ☐ yes   ☐ no

3. Does Arton circle the type of meat?   ☐ yes   ☐ no

4. Does Arton say what type of bread he wants? ☐ yes   ☐ no

C Read the sandwich form. Answer the questions.

Lunch for You
19 Prospect St.

Customer name: Walter Arakaki

Meat:
Tuna
Ham ✓
Chicken

Cheese:
American ✓
Cheddar
Swiss

Bread:
White Bread ✓
Wheat Bread
Roll

Condiments:
Mustard
Mayonnaise ✓
Ketchup

Vegetables:
Tomato ✓
Lettuce ✓
Onions ✓

1. What is the name of the deli?
   Lunch for You

2. What is the customer's name?
   _____

3. What kind of cheese does he want?
   _____

4. Does he want chicken?
   _____

5. Does he want a roll?
   _____

6. What kind of meat does he want?
   _____

D Write about you. Write what you like in the chart.

FOOD	WHAT I LIKE
Meat	
Cheese	
Vegetables	
Condiments	
Bread	

★ ★

TAKE IT OUTSIDE: Practice taking an order with a family member, friend, or coworker. Ask the questions. Check the answers on the order form.

1. What's your name?
2. What kind of meat do you want?
3. What kind of cheese do you want?
4. What kind of bread do you want?

★ ★

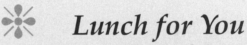

Lunch for You
19 Prospect St.
Arlington, VA 22201
(703) 555-8760

Customer name: _____

Meat:
Tuna
Ham
Chicken

Cheese:
American
Cheddar
Swiss

Bread:
White Bread
Wheat Bread
Roll

Condiments:
Mustard
Mayonnaise
Ketchup

Vegetables:
Tomato
Lettuce
Onions

Practice Test

DIRECTIONS: Answer the questions. Use the Answer Sheet.

1. Do you want white or wheat bread?

   A. White, please.

   B. Yes, I do.

   C. chicken

   D. a sandwich

2. Where's the cereal?

   A. Yes, we do.

   B. It's in Aisle 3.

   C. That's right.

   D. Thanks a lot.

3. How much is a can of tomatoes?

   A. That's a good price.

   B. That's expensive.

   C. It's in Aisle 4.

   D. $6.99

ANSWER SHEET				
1	A	B	C	D
2	A	B	C	D
3	A	B	C	D
4	A	B	C	D
5	A	B	C	D
6	A	B	C	D
7	A	B	C	D
8	A	B	C	D
9	A	B	C	D
10	A	B	C	D

DIRECTIONS: Look at the picture to answer the next 2 questions. Use the Answer Sheet.

4. How many eggs are there?

   A. 12

   B. 6

   C. $1.00

   D. 4

5. How much are the eggs?

   A. 12

   B. 6

   C. $1.00

   D. $.06

DIRECTIONS: Look at the food label to answer the next 3 questions. Use the Answer Sheet on page 90.

CHICKEN

NET WT	UNIT PRICE	SOLD ON
4.50	$1.99/LB	06/08/04

TOTAL PRICE
$8.96

6. How much does the package of chicken cost?

   A. $1.99

   B. $4.50

   C. $8.96

   D. $6.08

8. What date is on the package?

   A. 4.50

   B. $.199

   C. $8.96

   D. 6/08/04

7. How many pounds of chicken are in the package?

   A. 4.50

   B. 1.99

   C. 8.96

   D. 6.08

DIRECTIONS: Answer the questions. Use the Answer Sheet on page 90.

9. What can I get for you?

   A. A pound of cheese.

   B. Aisle 1.

   C. Yes, thank you.

   D. It's on sale.

10. What size is the can?

   A. extra large

   B. 15 ounces

   C. in Aisle 5

   D. $2.50

HOW DID YOU DO? Count the number of correct answers on your answer sheet. Record this number in the bar graph on the inside back cover.

What's your brother's name?

A Look at the family photo. Read the story. Write the words from the box on the lines.

husband	**wife**	**father**	**mother**
son	**daughter**	**niece**	**nephew**
brother	**sister**		

Elizabeth

This is a photo of everyone in Elizabeth's family. She has one child. She lives with her husband and her daughter in Westville. Her daughter is 16. Elizabeth's mother and father live in Westville, too. She sees them every day. Elizabeth's brother is married. She has a niece who is 2 years old.

B Check *true* or *false*.

1. Elizabeth has a son.   ☐ true ☑ false
2. She is married.   ☐ true ☐ false
3. Her mother lives near Elizabeth.   ☐ true ☐ false
4. Elizabeth has a sister.   ☐ true ☐ false
5. Elizabeth's brother has a son.   ☐ true ☐ false
6. Her daughter is 2 years old.   ☐ true ☐ false

C Complete the sentences. Write *do* or *does*.

1. _Does_ Elizabeth have a son?
2. _____ her parents live near her?
3. _____ Elizabeth have a granddaughter?
4. _____ they live in Westville?
5. _____ Elizabeth have a nephew?
6. _____ her husband live in Westville?

D Write the words in the correct order.

1. with/you/Do/live/parents/your
   _____ *Do you live with your parents* _____ ?

2. brother/Does/your/near/you/live
   _____ ?

3. Do/children/have/you
   _____ ?

4. grandfather/play/Does/your/cards
   _____ ?

5. alone/they/Do/live
   _____ ?

6. he/brothers/Does/have
   _____ ?

E Look at the chart. Write the number you have in your family.

FAMILY MEMBER	NUMBER	FAMILY MEMBER	NUMBER
mother		father	
sister		brother	
aunt		uncle	
daughter		son	
grandmother		grandfather	

2
LESSON

I usually cook dinner.

A Match the actions and things.

Actions	Things
1. pay	a. the dishes
2. make	b. the trash
3. take out	c. the bills
4. cook	d. the house
5. buy	e. the beds
6. clean	f. dinner
7. wash	g. the groceries

B Read the schedule and answer the questions.

CHORE	SUN.	MON.	TUES.	WED.	THURS.	FRI.	SAT.
cook dinner	M	C	K	M	C	K	all
wash dishes	C	K	M	C	K	M	all
take out trash	K	M	C	K	M	C	all

Madeline (M), Charmaine (C) and Kristina (K) are roommates. They live together in a house.
They work together to do the jobs in their home.

1. Who cooks dinner on Sunday? _____Madeline_____

2. Who washes dishes on Wednesday? _____

3. Who takes out the trash on Thursday? _____

4. Does Madeline cook dinner on Wednesday? _____

5. Does Kristina wash dishes on Tuesday? _____

6. Does Charmaine take out the trash on Sunday? _____

C Write the words in the correct place in the chart.

cook/cooks	make/makes	wash/washes
take/takes	buy/buys	clean/cleans
watch/watches	work/works	live/lives
tell/tells	read/reads	play/plays
go/goes	do/does	fix/fixes

simple present

+ S	+ ES
cook	wash

D Circle the correct words.

Everyone in my family helps at home. I (cook/cooks) dinner on Monday and Wednesday. My mother always (do/does) the laundry. My father (wash/washes) the dishes after dinner. My sisters (take/takes) out the trash. My brothers (clean/cleans) the house. We all (make/makes) our beds in the morning. My mother usually (pay/pays) the bills, but sometimes my father (do/does). (Do/Does) you help at home?

simple present

E Write about you. Who has each family responsibility in your home?

FAMILY RESPONSIBILITIES	WHO DOES IT?
Cook dinner	
Take out trash	
Pay the bills	
Clean the house	
Buy the groceries	

F Write about who does the chores in your home. Write complete sentences.

LESSON

What do you do for fun?

A Circle the correct answer.

1. Do you play cards?
   - Ⓐ Yes, often.
   - B. In the library.

2. Do you play an instrument?
   - A. I take pictures.
   - B. No, never.

3. Who in your family plays soccer?
   - A. Sometimes.
   - B. My sister.

4. Does your family tell stories?
   - A. Two or three.
   - B. Yes, often.

5. Do you listen to music?
   - A. Yes, sometimes.
   - B. Yes, you do.

6. Does your father read the newspaper?
   - A. Yes, he is.
   - B. Yes, he does.

B Write the words under the photos.

| play cards | listen to music | play soccer | read the newspaper |

_____

_____

_____   _____

C Write the actions in Activity B in the order you like them.

1. _____ ♥♥♥♥

2. _____ ♥♥♥

3. _____ ♥♥

4. _____ ♥

D Write these words on the lines below. One word can be used 2 times.

soccer	music	the story	cards
the book	the newspaper	the teacher	an instrument

_____   _____ soccer _____
            (**play**)
                      _____

_____   _____
            (**listen to**)
                      _____

_____
            (**read**)
                      _____

Family Portraits

A Complete the sentences.

ACROSS

1. My son's daughter is my _____.
4. My father's wife is my _____.
5. My mother's husband is my _____.
6. My grandfather is my grandmother's _____.

DOWN

1. My mother's father is my _____.
2. My father's sister is my _____.
3. My brother's son is my _____.

B Write the words in the crossword puzzle below.

C Circle the word that is different in each row.

1. mother	aunt	(cards)
2. father	dishes	brother
3. story	clean	wash
4. pay	son	buy
5. cook	clean	cards
6. wash	read	listen

D Complete the sentences. Write *don't* or *doesn't*.

I <u>have</u> a brother.	I <u>don't have</u> a sister.
We <u>live</u> in Westville.	We <u>don't live</u> in Madison.
You <u>wash</u> the dishes.	You <u>don't cook</u> dinner.
They <u>play</u> soccer.	They don't <u>play</u> cards
He <u>listens</u> to the radio.	He <u>doesn't read</u> the newspaper.
She <u>pays</u> the bills.	She <u>doesn't buy</u> the groceries.

1. I _____*don't*_____ live here.

2. He _____ have a book.

3. They _____ clean the house.

4. Maria _____ like apples.

5. Fernando and I _____ wash the dishes.

6. You _____ read the newspaper.

7. My parents _____ live with me.

8. My sister _____ work.

9. My aunt and uncle _____ play cards.

10. Ahmed _____ play soccer.

11. We _____ cook dinner.

E Complete the story about Brigitte's family.

My mother _____ (clean) our house. She _____ (clean, not) every day because she _____ (work) too. My father _____ (drive) a bus. He _____ (go) to work Monday through Friday. I _____ (take) out the trash. My brother _____ (cook) dinner. My sister _____ (do, not) anything. She is a baby. My grandmother and grandfather _____ (live) with us. They _____ (go, not) to school or to work. My grandmother _____ (listen) to music. My grandfather _____ (read) the newspaper. We _____ (play, not) cards, but we _____ (play) soccer.

F Write about your family.

_____

_____

99

I'd like an application for membership.

A Read Martin Costa's application to join an organization. Write the information.

Name: Martin Costa

Mailing Address: 32 Hampstead St.

City: Monroe

State: NC

Zip: 28232

Home: (704) 555-9023

Business: (704) 555-6444

Gender: ● Male ○ Female

Date of Birth: 2 / 1 / 62

Marital Status: ● Married ○ Single

1. Martin's address: _____
2. His son's name: _____
3. His wife's birth date: _____
4. His daughter's age: _____
5. Martin's home phone number: (_____)_____
6. His mother's name: _____

Fill out this portion of the application if other members of your family are included in this membership. (Must be eligible as a dependent on your Federal Income Tax forms.)

Name 1: Sarah Costa

Gender: ○ Male ● Female

Date of Birth: 4 / 15 / 65

Relationship: wife

Name 2: Thomas Costa

Gender: ● Male ○ Female

Date of Birth: 8 / 12 / 89

Relationship: son

Name 3: Hannah Costa

Gender: ○ Male ● Female

Date of Birth: 4 / 22 / 92

Relationship: daughter

Name 4: Laura Costa

Gender: ○ Male ● Female

Date of Birth: 12 / 13 / 32

Relationship: mother

B Write the names, ages, and relationships of the members of the Costa family.

NAME	AGE	RELATIONSHIP
Martin Costa		_____

C Check *yes* or *no*.

1. Martin has two daughters.   ☐ yes ☑ no
2. His wife's name is Hannah.   ☐ yes ☐ no
3. There are three females in his family.   ☐ yes ☐ no
4. He has a son.   ☐ yes ☐ no
5. Martin's birthday is February 2.   ☐ yes ☐ no
6. Martin is single.   ☐ yes ☐ no

D Complete the application for you.

Name: _____   Home telephone: _____

Address: _____

City: _____   State: _____   Zip: _____

Birth date: ___/___/___   Gender: ○ male   ○ female

OTHER FAMILY MEMBERS

NAME	BIRTH DATE	GENDER (M/F)	RELATIONSHIP

Signature: _____

★ ★

TAKE IT OUTSIDE: Go to a community center, recreation center, or gym near your house and get an application. Bring it to class. List the information you need to write on the application (e.g., name, address).

★ ★

I need to take family leave.

A Read the definition. Use the words from the box to complete the definitions below.

> **family leave:** workers can take time off, or leave, from the job to take care of their families (U.S. Family and Medical Leave Act of 1993). This law (for companies with 50 or more workers and employees with at least a year of service) gives 12 weeks of leave a year for family medical emergencies and for the birth of a child. The company can not take the worker's job away if the worker takes this time off from work to take care of his or her family.

---

medical emergency   family leave
U. S. Family and Medical Leave Act of 1993

---

1. _____ : a law that says workers can take time off from work for family needs

2. _____ : the time a worker doesn't work so he or she can care for family

3. _____ : when someone gets sick or gets hurt

B Circle the correct answer.

1. The U.S. Family and Medical Leave Act of 1993 gives _____ weeks of leave a year.

   A. 2   B. 8   C. 12

2. Workers at companies with _____ employees or more can take leave.

   A. 15   B. 50   C. 500

3. Workers can take leave when _____ .

   A. they go on a trip   B. they have a financial emergency   C. a family member gets sick or hurt

4. To get family leave, workers must have their jobs for at least _____ .

   A. two months   B. six months   C. one year

C Read the conversation. Write *Rick* or *Tony* on the lines.

Tony: Excuse me, Rick, can I talk to you?

Rick: Sure, Tony. What is it?

Tony: My mother lives with me and she is 80 years old. I take care of her. Last week she hurt her back. She can't walk, she can't cook, she can't do anything.

Rick: That's terrible. I'm so sorry. How can I help?

Tony: Well, I think I need to take some family leave to take care of her.

Rick: Okay. How much time do you need?

Tony: Maybe 6 weeks.

Rick: Okay. It will be hard without you, but you should help your mother. When does the leave start?

Tony: I'm working this week. My sister is here to help, too. Then next week, I'm taking leave. Thanks, Rick.

1. _____*Rick*_____ is the supervisor.

2. _____ needs to take family leave.

3. _____ takes care of his mother.

4. _____ says "I'm so sorry."

5. _____'s sister is here to help.

6. _____ works with Tony.

D Answer the questions.

1. Why is Tony taking family leave? _____

2. Where does Tony's mother live? _____

3. What is her age? _____

4. How much leave does Tony need? _____

5. When does the leave start? _____

★ ★

TAKE IT OUTSIDE: Ask your supervisor for a description of your family leave policy, or ask a family member or friend to get a description from his or her supervisor. Bring it to class.

★ ★

Practice Test

DIRECTIONS: Read the form to answer the next 5 questions. Use the Answer Sheet.

Name: _____ Line 1

Mailing Address: _____ Line 2

City: _____

State: _____

Zip: _____

Home: _____

Business: _____

Gender: ○ Male   ○ Female   Line 3

Date of Birth: [____] / [____] / [____]

Marital Status: ○ Married   ○ Single   Line 4

Name 1: _____ Line 5

Gender: ○ Male   ○ Female

Date of Birth: [____] / [____] / [____]

Relationship: _____ Line 6

Terry Coggins lives at 3902 West Peach St. She is single. She has a daughter. Her daughter's name is Pamela.

1. On what line do you put *single*?
   A. Line 1
   B. Line 2
   C. Line 3
   D. Line 4

2. On what line do you write *Terry Coggins*?
   A. Line 1
   B. Line 2
   C. Line 3
   D. Line 4

3. On what line do you mark *female*?
   A. Line 1
   B. Line 2
   C. Line 3
   D. Line 4

4. On what line do you write *daughter*?
   A. Line 3
   B. Line 4
   C. Line 5
   D. Line 6

5. On what line do you write *Pamela Coggins*?
   A. Line 3
   B. Line 4
   C. Line 5
   D. Line 6

ANSWER SHEET

1 Ⓐ Ⓑ Ⓒ Ⓓ
2 Ⓐ Ⓑ Ⓒ Ⓓ
3 Ⓐ Ⓑ Ⓒ Ⓓ
4 Ⓐ Ⓑ Ⓒ Ⓓ
5 Ⓐ Ⓑ Ⓒ Ⓓ
6 Ⓐ Ⓑ Ⓒ Ⓓ
7 Ⓐ Ⓑ Ⓒ Ⓓ
8 Ⓐ Ⓑ Ⓒ Ⓓ
9 Ⓐ Ⓑ Ⓒ Ⓓ
10 Ⓐ Ⓑ Ⓒ Ⓓ

DIRECTIONS: Answer the questions. Use the Answer Sheet on page 104.

6. What is her relationship?
   A. male
   B. sister
   C. play cards
   D. Mexican

7. What do they do for fun?
   A. tell stories
   B. take out the trash
   C. parents
   D. bus driver

8. What do you pay?
   A. dinner
   B. the dishes
   C. the bills
   D. the laundry

9. How often do you play cards?
   A. in my house
   B. sometimes
   C. with my brother
   D. Yes, I do.

10. Where does your uncle live?
    A. in California
    B. his wife and children
    C. She is here.
    D. never

HOW DID YOU DO? Count the number of correct answers on your answer sheet. Record this number in the bar graph on the inside back cover.

Spotlight: Grammar

SIMPLE PRESENT STATEMENTS		
Regular verbs I You **work** in a hospital. We **don't work** in a library. They	He **works** in an office. She **doesn't work** in a bank.	
Irregular verbs I You **go to school**. We **don't go** to work. They	He **goes** to school. She **doesn't go** to work.	

A Complete the sentences. Write *don't* or *doesn't*.

1. My sister pays the bills. She _____ wash the dishes.

2. I go to work at 7:00 A.M. I _____ go home until 5:00 P.M.

3. My parents live in New York. They _____ live near me.

4. We read every evening. We _____ watch TV.

5. You eat a lot of bananas. You _____ eat a lot of avocados.

6. Tim has a sister. He _____ have a brother.

B Complete the sentences. Use the verbs in parentheses.

1. I ____*like*____ wearing pants. They're good for work. I ____*don't like*____ wearing dresses. (like)

2. Gina _____ two sisters. Their names are Linda and Grace. She _____ brothers. (have)

3. They _____ to school in the morning. Their class is at 9:00 A.M. They _____ to work in the morning. They work from 3:00–11:00 P.M. (go)

4. My mother _____ the bills. She is good with numbers. My father _____ the bills. He can't add. (pay)

106

INFORMATION QUESTIONS WITH THE SIMPLE PRESENT

What		I need for school?	What		he need for school?
Where		you live?	Where		she live?
When	**do**	they usually leave?	When	**does**	it usually leave?
Why		you live there?	Why		he live there?
Who		we live with?	Who		she live with?
How many sisters		they have?	How many sisters		your mother have?

C Check the correct answer.

1. What do you want for dinner?

   ☐ Yes, I do.   ☐ I want fish.

2. Where does your sister live?

   ☐ No, she doesn't.   ☐ She lives in Omaha.

3. When does he go to work?

   ☐ at 7:00 A.M.   ☐ at the bank

4. Do you have sisters?

   ☐ Yes, I do.   ☐ No, you don't.

5. Who do they like?

   ☐ Mac Everland   ☐ chicken

D Complete the questions. Write *do* or *does*. Then answer the questions.

1. How many hours _____ you work?

   _____

2. Who _____ your teacher live with?

   _____

3. Where _____ your parents live?

   _____

4. When _____ the class start?

   _____

5. What _____ your family eat for breakfast?

   _____

6. How much _____ a shirt cost?

   _____

LESSON 1

Head, Shoulders, Knees, and Toes

A Write the words from the box on the lines.

| head | shoulder | arm | elbow | hand | leg | knee | back | foot | ankle |

B Make words from the letters.

| wrist | neck ✓ | chest | stomach |
| finger | nose | mouth | throat |

EXAMPLE: cekn   *neck*

1. grnife   _____
2. htarot   _____
3. sriwt   _____
4. hotamsc   _____
5. ohtmu   _____
6. thsec   _____
7. soen   _____

C Check *yes* or *no*.

1. People can fly.	☐ yes	☑ no
2. Books can talk.	☐ yes	☐ no
3. Teachers can read.	☐ yes	☐ no
4. Librarians can check out books.	☐ yes	☐ no
5. Computers can cook.	☐ yes	☐ no
6. Children can play soccer.	☐ yes	☐ no

D Answer the questions about you and your family. Use *can* and *can't*.

1. Can you cook?   _____ Yes, I can. _____

2. Can your mother play soccer?   _____

3. Can your father stand on one foot?   _____

4. Can you and your family go to the library? _____

5. Can you drive a car?   _____

6. Can you say the time?   _____

7. Can you write your name?   _____

8. Can you stand on your head?   _____

E Write the words in the correct order.

1. you/Can/your toes/touch

   _____ Can you touch your toes _____?

2. read/a book/in English/can/I

   _____.

3. They/drive/to school/can

   _____.

4. can/to the store/We/go

   _____.

5. cook/dinner/he/Can

   _____?

6. Giovanna/go/Can/to school

   _____?

I have a bad headache.

A Match the questions and answers.

Nurse's Questions	Patient's Answers
1. What's the problem?	a. No, I don't think so.
2. Does your knee hurt, too?	b. I have an earache.
3. Is it broken?	c. Yes, I can.
4. Can you touch your toes?	d. No, it doesn't.

B Circle the correct answer.

1. What's the problem with Matt?

   A. Matt Harper   B. He has a bad headache.

2. Does your back hurt, too?

   A. No, it doesn't.   B. I have a stomachache.

3. Is it broken?

   A. No, I don't think so.   B. I have a fever.

4. I have a sore throat.

   A. Does your finger hurt, too?   B. Does your head hurt, too?

5. Can you stand on one foot?

   A. No, I can't.   B. That's right.

C Write the problem under the picture.

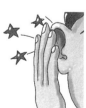   

1. _____   2. _____

3. _____   4. _____

D Read the medical history form. Write the information.

Pineville Family Physicians
Medical History

Name: __Peppers__   __Barbara__   __Ann__   Birth Date: __10/17/78__
              Last   First   Middle

Home Address: __1953 Tompkins St.__   __Pineville__   __SD__   __28134__
                          Street Address   City   State   Zip Code

Insurance Information:
Are you covered by insurance?   ☑ yes   ☐ no

If yes, what provider? __Health Plus__

GENERAL QUESTIONS
Do you have a problem with:

    1. headaches?   ☑ yes   ☐ no

    2. stomachaches?   ☐ yes   ☑ no

    3. backaches?   ☐ yes   ☑ no

    4. earaches?   ☑ yes   ☐ no

    5. sore throats?   ☐ yes   ☑ no

    6. fevers?   ☐ yes   ☑ no

Reason for visit: ___a terrible cough___

1. Patient's Name: _____

2. Birth Date: _____

3. Problems: _____

4. Insurance Company: _____

5. Reason for visit: _____

E Answer the questions about you.

1. How often do you get headaches?   _____

2. Do you sometimes get a sore throat?   _____

3. Do you have a stomachache today?   _____

3 LESSON

Put ice on it.

A Complete the remedies. Use the words from the box.

1. Put _____*heat*_____ on it.

2. Take cough _____.

3. Keep it _____.

4. Eat soft _____.

5. Drink _____.

6. Use _____.

> medicine
> dry
> liquids
> ear drops
> heat
> food

B Read the letters. Underline the problems.

Dear Dr. Dina, **(greeting)**
I get terrible headaches. I can't work or go to school when I have a headache. Help!
　　　　　(closing)　Sincerely,
　　　　　(name)　Sick Susan

Dear Sick Susan,
See your doctor first. Sometimes you can take aspirin or rest to help a headache. Good luck!
　　　　　Sincerely,
　　　　　Dr. Dina

Dr. Dina,
My son has a backache. He hurt it in soccer. He feels terrible. What should I do?
　　　　　Sincerely,
　　　　　Worried Mom

Dear Worried Mom,
I think your son will be fine. He should put heat on it and rest. Call the doctor if he is not okay tomorrow.
　　　　　Sincerely,
　　　　　Dr. Dina

Dr. Dina,
My mother has a fever. She also has a cough and a runny nose. I want to help.
What can I do?
　　　　　Sincerely,
　　　　　A Daughter
　　　　　in Mashburn

Dear Daughter in Mashburn,
Your mother can take aspirin for her fever. She should rest in bed and drink a lot of liquids. You are a good daughter to take care of your mother.
　　　　　Sincerely,
　　　　　Dr. Dina

C Match the problems with Dr. Dina's advice.

Problems

1. headache

2. backache

3. fever, cough, and runny nose

Dr. Dina's Advice

a. See a doctor, rest, and take aspirin.

b. Take aspirin, rest, and drink liquids.

c. Put heat on it, rest, and call the doctor.

D Write a letter to Dr. Dina. Look at the first letter in Activity B for ideas.

_____, (greeting)

_____

_____

_____

(closing)   _____

(your name) _____

E Write the sentences in the correct place in the chart.

should/shouldn't

See a doctor every year.   Play with your children.
Do your homework.   Drive a car without a driver's license.
Watch TV every day.   Use ear drops for a headache.
Sleep in class.   Eat healthy food.
Read to your children.   Eat ice cream for every meal.

THINGS YOU *SHOULD* DO	THINGS YOU *SHOULDN'T* DO

F Make the sentences negative.

1. You should go to bed.   _____You shouldn't go to bed._____

should/shouldn't

2. He should see a doctor. _____

3. We should have a party. _____

4. They should pay the bill. _____

5. She should be late.   _____

6. I should eat dinner.   _____

113

LESSON 4

Safety Warnings

A Learn new words. Find and circle these words in the labels.

avoid	contains	heat	flush

CLEAR GLASS **CLEANER**

Directions: Spray and wipe surface to clean. **Caution:** Contains ammonia. Avoid contact with eyes. In case of eye contact, flush with water. Do not take internally. 64 oz.

ANTS OUT! KILLS ANTS

Caution: Avoid contact with eyes, skin, or clothes. Wash with soap and water after using. Do not take internally.

Flammable: Keep away from heat and out of reach of children.

24 oz.

CHLOR-UP *CLEANER* 2pt.

Warning: Contains bleach. Avoid contact with eyes. Do not use or mix with other cleaners, especially those with ammonia. Keep out of reach of children.

B Complete the sentences.

1. Clear Glass Cleaner contains _____*ammonia*_____.

2. Chlor-up Cleaner contains _____.

3. Ants Out is flammable. You should keep it away from _____.

4. You should avoid contact with eyes when using _____.

5. If you get Clear Glass Cleaner in your eyes, _____ with water.

6. Don't get Ants Out on your eyes, skin, or _____.

C Check *true* or *false*.

1. You can keep Ants Out near heat.

   ☐ true   ☑ false

2. You can drink the 3 products in Activity A.

   ☐ true   ☐ false

3. You should keep Chlor-up Cleaner away from children.

   ☐ true   ☐ false

4. You shouldn't use Chlor-up Cleaner with Clear Glass Cleaner.

   ☐ true   ☐ false

5. You should wash with soap and water after using Ants Out.

   ☐ true   ☐ false

6. You should keep everything in the kitchen.

   ☐ true   ☐ false

D Write the amounts another way.

> **1 gallon (gal.) = 4 quarts (qt.)**
> **1 quart (qt.) = 2 pints (pt.)**
> **1 pint (pt.) = 2 cups (c.) = 16 fluid ounces (fl. oz)**

1. 64 ounces = _____ gallon(s)

2. 2 gallons = _____ pints

3. 10 pints = _____ quarts

4. 32 ounces = _____ cups

5. 8 cups = _____ quarts

E Use the information from Activities A and D to complete the chart.

PRODUCT	OUNCES	PINTS
Clear Glass Cleaner	*64* oz	
Ants Out		
Chlor-up Cleaner		

My hand hurts.

A Learn new words. Find and circle these words in the story.

injury	place	supervisor	accident

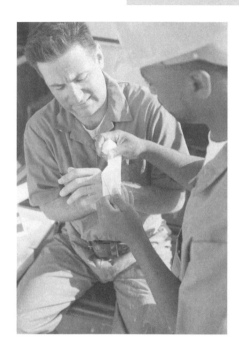

      Peter Banks is a single man. He works in construction. He builds houses and other buildings. Today, he is cutting some wood on the first floor of a new bank, and he has an accident at work. At 1:17, he cuts his hand. His hand hurts. Howard Miller is Peter's supervisor. He is putting a bandage on Peter's hand. Peter and Howard fill out an accident/injury report form. The place Peter and Howard are working at is First Market Bank, 100 Center Street. The date today is July 23.

B Answer the questions. Use the words from the box above.

1. What is the problem?   = _____ *accident* _____
2. Where?   = _____
3. What is hurt?   = _____
4. Who is the boss?   = _____

C Check *yes* or *no*.

1. Peter has an accident.   ☑ yes   ☐ no
2. Howard has an injury.   ☐ yes   ☐ no
3. Peter has an injury.   ☐ yes   ☐ no
4. Peter cuts his hand.   ☐ yes   ☐ no
5. Peter and Howard work in a bank.   ☐ yes   ☐ no
6. Howard is Peter's supervisor.   ☐ yes   ☐ no

D Complete the form about Peter's accident.

Name of employee:_____ Date of birth: _05/19/68_

Address: _1611 Forest Street_ City: _Stanton_ State:_TN_ Zip: _38069_ ⟵ Line 1

Sex: ☐ male ☐ female Marital status: ☐ single ☐ married ☐ divorced

Occupation:_____

Date of accident:_____ Time of accident:_____ ⟵ Line 2

Place of the accident:_____ ⟵ Line 3

Type of injury: ☐ bruise ☐ burn ☐ cut ☐ fracture ☐ sprain

Body part injured: ☐ ankle ☐ arm ☐ back ☐ chest ☐ finger } Line 4

   ☐ hand ☐ head ☐ ear ☐ eye ☐ leg

Employee signature:_____ ⟵ Line 5

Supervisor's signature:_____ ⟵ Line 6

E Write the number of the line in Activity D next to the information.

1. Where do you write the date of the accident? ___Line 2___
2. On what line should you write where the accident was? _____
3. On what line should you check "hand"? _____
4. On what line should you write "1:17 P.M."? _____
5. On what line do you write Peter's address? _____
6. Where should Peter sign his name? _____

TAKE IT OUTSIDE: Interview a family member, friend, or coworker about a time he or she hurt something. Complete the form about it.

Name:_____ Date of birth:_____

Address:_____ City:_____ State:____ Zip:_____

Sex: ☐ male ☐ female Marital status: ☐ single ☐ married ☐ divorced

Occupation:_____

Date of accident:_____ Time of accident:_____

Type of injury:_____

Lin is at the doctor's office.

A Write the letter of the photo next to the sentence.

1. The doctor is looking at Lin's ears. _____

2. The doctor is listening to Lin's back. _____

3. The doctor is looking at Lin's eyes. _____

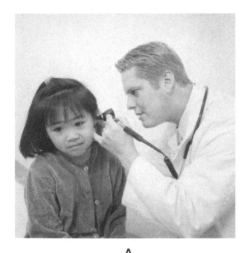

A

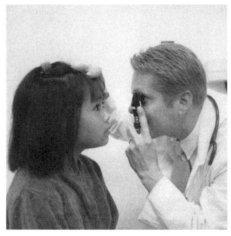

B

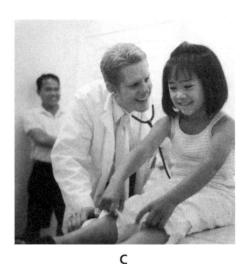

C

Lin is at the doctor's office. The doctor is looking at her ears and her eyes. He is giving Lin an exam. Lin is going to school next week. The doctor says Lin is okay to go to school. Her eyes and her ears are good. Lin is going to the dentist next. The dentist checks Lin's teeth.

B Answer the questions.

1. Where is Lin?   _____

2. What does the doctor look at?   _____

3. Where is Lin going next?   _____

C Learn new words. Find and circle the words in the notice on page 119.

offer	exam	immunization	discount	income

Eye, Ear and Dental Exams for School

The **Parker County Health Department** offers the exams for $12. The department also provides immunizations.

The **Stanly County Health Department** will offer special hours for exams in August before the start of school. For information on the Downing clinic, call (706) 555-1318; for the Rivertown clinic, call (706) 555-3727; for the Hawkins/Medford clinic, call (706) 555-3331. Exams cost $15, but you can ask for a discount based on income and family size.

The **Burke County Health Department** offers exams. The cost of the exam is based on income. Walk-in patients are seen only on Mondays. Patients must have appointments on Tuesdays and Wednesdays. No exams on Thursdays and Fridays. Call (706) 555-1740.

D Write a word from the box in Activity C next to the meaning.

1. money earned in a year = _____
2. lower price = _____
3. medicine to prevent sickness, in a shot = _____
4. give, have = _____
5. when a doctor checks/looks at a patient = _____

E Match the questions and answers.

Questions	Answers
1. What is the phone number for the Rivertown clinic?	a. Tuesdays and Wednesdays
2. What days do you need an appointment at the Burke County clinic?	b. Three
3. How much are exams at the Parker County Health Department?	c. August
4. What month does the Stanly County Health Department offer special hours?	d. $12
5. How many clinics does Stanly County have?	e. (706) 555-3727
6. What is the phone number for Burke County?	f. (706) 555-1740

★ ★

TAKE IT OUTSIDE: Interview 2 people in your family, neighborhood, or workplace. Write the information in the chart.

NAME	DATE OF LAST EYE EXAM (MONTH/YR)	DATE OF LAST EAR EXAM (MONTH/YEAR)	DATE OF LAST DENTAL EXAM (MONTH/YEAR)

★ ★

Practice Test

DIRECTIONS: Look at the label to answer the next 5 questions. Use the Answer Sheet.

1. What does Extra Bright contain?
   A. bleach
   B. ammonia
   C. flammable
   D. large loads

2. You should avoid contact with:
   A. skin
   B. eyes
   C. washer
   D. water

ANSWER SHEET				
1	A	B	C	D
2	A	B	C	D
3	A	B	C	D
4	A	B	C	D
5	A	B	C	D
6	A	B	C	D
7	A	B	C	D
8	A	B	C	D
9	A	B	C	D
10	A	B	C	D

3. You have young children. Where should you keep Extra Bright?
   A. in their bedroom
   B. under the kitchen sink
   C. in a locked cabinet
   D. in a place that's easy to reach

4. You should not use Extra Bright with:
   A. clothes
   B. children
   C. hot water
   D. ammonia

Directions to clean clothes:
Fill cap to line. Add to washer. Use more for large loads. Wash as usual. Works in hot or cold water.

Caution: Contains bleach. Avoid contact with eyes. In case of eye contact, flush with water. Do not use with ammonia.

Keep out of reach of children.

5. You got Extra Bright in your eyes. What should you do?
   A. Call the doctor.
   B. Avoid contact.
   C. Flush with water.
   D. Lie down.

DIRECTIONS: Look at the form to answer the next 5 questions. Use the Answer Sheet on page 120.

Name of employee:_____①_____ Date of birth:_____

Address:_____ City:_____ State:_____ Zip:_____

Sex: ☐ male ☐ female   Marital status: ☐ single ☐ married ☐ divorced

Occupation:_____②_____

Date of accident:____③_____ Time of the accident:____④_____

Place of the accident:_____⑤_____

Type of injury: ☐ bruise   ☐ burn   ☐ cut   ☐ fracture   ☐ sprain ⑥

Body part injured: ☐ ankle   ☐ arm   ☐ back   ☐ chest   ☐ finger ⑦

                   ☐ hand   ☐ head   ☐ ear   ☐ eye   ☐ leg

Employee signature:_____

---

6. Tom had an accident. He injured his finger. Where does he check "finger"?

   A. space 1   B. space 3

   C. space 5   D. space 7

7. Dotty cut her leg. Where does she check "cut"?

   A. space 2   B. space 4

   C. space 6   D. space 8

8. Where do you write that the accident is at 2:30 P.M.?

   A. space 2   B. space 4

   C. space 6   D. space 8

9. Mrs. Moony had an accident on October 5, 2004. Where do you write the date?

   A. space 1   B. space 3

   C. space 5   D. space 7

10. Where do you write the person's name?

   A. space 1   B. space 3

   C. space 5   D. space 7

HOW DID YOU DO? Count the number of correct answers on your answer sheet. Record this number in the bar graph on the inside back cover.

Their new house has 3 bedrooms.

A Write about your home. Write the words in the correct place(s) in the chart.

bathtub	bed	table	sofa
bookcase	stove	refrigerator	closet
lamp	dresser	carpet	toilet
cabinet	smoke alarm	shower	chair

BATHROOM	BEDROOM	DINING ROOM	KITCHEN	LIVING ROOM
bathtub				

B Circle *true* or *false*.

1. There is a bookcase in the room.

   (true)   false

2. There is a lamp in the room.

   true   false

3. There isn't a sofa.

   true   false

4. There is a table.

   true   false

5. It is a kitchen.

   true   false

6. There aren't any people in the room.

   true   false

C Write about the room in Activity B. Use *There is/isn't* and *There are/aren't.*

This room is a _____

_____

_____

D Complete the sentences. Write *has, have,* or *had.*

1. I *have* a new car. My old car *had* a lot of problems.

2. Last year, Maria _____ an accident.

3. He _____ a headache today.

4. Their new house _____ 3 bedrooms.

5. Our teacher this year _____ brown hair.

6. Our teacher last year _____ blond hair.

comparing past and present

E Circle the correct words.

1. Last week I (am / (was)) sick.

2. Today (is / was) Friday.

3. Yesterday (is / was) Sunday.

4. We (are / were) late to work last night.

5. They (are / were) in the library now.

6. In our old apartment, the table (is / was) in the living room.

comparing past and present

F Write the words in the correct order.

1. a cabinet/There/in his kitchen/is

   _____

2. has/My bathroom/a shower

   _____

3. is/in Mandy's bedroom/The bed

   _____

4. four smoke detectors/are/in my house/There

   _____

2
LESSON

The Lees' old house had a garage.

A Look at the photo. Check the things you see.

- ❑ fireplace
- ❑ pool
- ❑ garden
- ❑ garage
- ❑ carport
- ❑ yard
- ❑ driveway
- ❑ patio

B Match the things and the places.

Things	Places
1. fire	a. garage
2. car	b. patio
3. flowers	c. yard
4. grass	d. pool
5. chairs	e. fireplace
6. water	f. garden

C Complete the sentences. Use the words from Activity B.

1. You can put your _____*car*_____ in your garage.

2. You can plant _____ in your garden.

3. You can mow _____ in your yard.

4. You can have _____ on your patio.

5. You can have a _____ in your fireplace

6. You should put _____ in your pool.

D Circle the correct answer.

1. Where is the car?
   - (A.) It's in the garage.
   - B. It's in the fireplace.

2. Where are the flowers?
   - A. They're in the pool.
   - B. They're in the garden.

3. Do you want a pool?
   - A. Yes, I do.
   - B. Yes, it does.

4. Does your home have a fireplace?
   - A. In the garage.
   - B. Yes, it does.

5. Where is the pool?
   - A. On the second floor.
   - B. In the backyard.

6. What do you want in your dream house?
   - A. a fireplace
   - B. Yes, I do.

E Write 3 sentences about your home.

EXAMPLE: My home has a ___driveway___. It doesn't have a ___garage___.

1. _____
2. _____
3. _____

F Check *yes* or *no*.

1289 Tynedale St., Linden

Move in now and enjoy this four-bedroom home. Formal living room with fireplace, dining room, kitchen with breakfast area, three baths, and two-car garage.

Open House
Come and see it!

Today   **2:00–4:00 P.M.**
          (605) 555-5440

1. There is a fireplace.
   ☐ yes   ☐ no

2. It has 5 bedrooms.
   ☐ yes   ☐ no

3. It has 3 bathrooms.
   ☐ yes   ☐ no

4. There is a garage.
   ☐ yes   ☐ no

5. People can see the house at 2:00 P.M.
   ☐ yes   ☐ no

He fell down the stairs.

A Write the past form of the verbs.

1. fall _____
2. slip _____
3. cut _____
4. like _____
5. get _____

6. need _____
7. work _____
8. hurt _____
9. want _____
10. trip _____

B Write the past form of the verbs in the correct place in the chart.

REGULAR PAST FORMS	IRREGULAR PAST FORMS

C Complete the sentences. Use the past form of the verbs in Activity A.

1. I can't come to work today. I _____*hurt*_____ my back.
2. He needs a bandage. He _____ his hand and it's bleeding.
3. She _____ a new job last month and really likes it.
4. They _____ on the project for 12 hours yesterday.
5. You _____ down the stairs last night.
6. How many people _____ on the wet floor yesterday?

D Match the questions and answers.

Questions

1. What happened to Kathy?
2. Is he okay now?
3. What happened to the Martins?
4. How many people got hurt at the game yesterday?
5. What happened to Peter?

Answers

a. They fell down the stairs.
b. Yes, I think so.
c. He cut his hand with a knife.
d. Three.
e. She slipped in the shower.

E Learn new words. Find and circle the words in the reading.

bicycle   helmet   rugs   toys   tape   protect

A

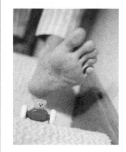

B

Keep your children safe: Prevent accidents

Follow these steps to protect your child from falls:

1. Don't put chairs near windows.
2. Close and lock windows when children are alone in the room.
3. Put tape on rugs and carpet so they can't slip.
4. Keep toys and other things away from your stairs.
5. Tell your child to wear a helmet when riding a bicycle.

F Write the number of the step that matches the photo.

A: Step _____   B: Step _____

G Check *yes* or *no*.

1. You should put toys on the stairs. ☐ yes ☐ no
2. You shouldn't have chairs near windows. ☐ yes ☐ no
3. You should put tape on rugs and carpet so they don't slip. ☐ yes ☐ no
4. Children shouldn't wear helmets when they ride bicycles. ☐ yes ☐ no
5. You should close windows when children are alone in the room. ☐ yes ☐ no

H Write 1 thing you do to prevent accidents at your home.

_____

LESSON 4

Housing Ads

A Find these words in the puzzle. Circle them.

1. stove ✓
2. bed
3. toilet
4. apartment
5. condo
6. lamp
7. sofa
8. closet
9. yard
10. patio
11. garage
12. pool
13. sink
14. room

```
s   i   n   k   c   s   t   o   v   e
g   t   o   i   l   e   t   h   u   l
s   n   f   p   o   o   l   a   m   p
o   p   o   t   s   v   w   c   k   m
f   a   y   b   e   d   m   o   p   r
a   p   a   r   t   m   e   n   t   o
g   a   r   a   g   e   y   d   i   o
z   b   d   p   a   t   i   o   a   m
```

B Match the abbreviations and the words.

Abbreviations	Words
1. apt	a. month
2. bth	b. apartment
3. bed	c. garage
4. gar	d. bathroom
5. nr	e. near
6. mo	f. bedroom

C Complete the sentences. Use the simple past form of the verb in parentheses.

1. I _____bought_____ (buy) a car last week.

2. She _____ (need) a new coat.

3. We _____ (have) a good time at the party.

4. Nick _____ (be) in school yesterday.

5. You _____ (call) me.

6. They _____ (like) the movie.

D Rewrite the sentences using the negative form of the verb.

1. Tamara liked the party.
   Tamara didn't like the party.

2. Sammy wanted a banana.
   _____

3. We worked very hard yesterday.
   _____

4. They needed books for class.
   _____

5. You got hurt in the game.
   _____

6. I fell off the ladder.
   _____

E Write 3 things you did and 3 things you didn't do yesterday, last week, or last year.

1. _I bought a new shirt last week. I didn't buy a new dress._

2. _____

3. _____

4. _____

Wear protective equipment.

A Learn new words. Find and circle the words in the reading.

harness	protective equipment	ear plugs	machinery
hard hat	coveralls	safety glasses	gloves

Safety Rules

1. Do not wear loose clothing around machinery.

2. Wear protective equipment: safety glasses, ear plugs, gloves, hard hat, coveralls, and harness when necessary.

3. Wear appropriate clothing and shoes.

4. Fire doors and aisles must be clear. Do not block aisles or exits with boxes.

5. No running.

6. Clean up spilled liquid and oil.

7. Turn off machines when you are not using them.

B Match the protective equipment and the body parts.

Protective Equipment   **Body Parts**

1. safety glasses   a. ears

2. harness   b. whole body

3. coveralls   c. eyes

4. hard hat   d. hands

5. gloves   e. head

6. ear plugs   f. back

C Complete the sentences. Use the words from the box.

| slip | fall | cut | hurt | leave |

1. You should clean up spilled liquid or oil so you don't _____ on the wet floor.
2. Workers need to keep the exits and aisles clear so people can _____ the building.
3. People wear hard hats because something could _____ on their heads.
4. Workers should wear harnesses when they lift heavy things or they can _____ their backs.
5. Sometimes workers _____ their hands on the machines.

D Circle the correct words.

Last week, Rita (slip / slipped) on the floor at work. There (is / was) some oil on the floor. She (hurt / fell) her back. Rita (is / was) better now. She (is / was) back at work. Her supervisor (has / had) a meeting yesterday with all the workers. Now everyone (is / was) careful. All the workers (clean up / work) water on the floor.

E Write about you. Write a story about a time you got hurt. Answer these questions.

1. What happened to you?
2. When did you get hurt?
3. Where did you get hurt?
4. What did you do?

_____

_____

_____

_____

_____

★ ★

TAKE IT OUTSIDE: Interview a family member, friend, or coworker. Ask the question. Write the answer. What is 1 safety rule you have at work or school?

_____

★ ★

COMMUNITY LESSON

Know your rights!

A Read the information below. What do you think "housing discrimination" is? Write a definition.

housing discrimination:_____

_____

Know your rights!

Mark and Karen Simone wanted to rent this house, but the rental office said no. Mark and Karen think that it was because they are from Africa. They got help from the Fair Housing Office. Housing discrimination is unfair.

Federal law prohibits housing discrimination because of your race, color, nationality, religion, sex, family status, or disability. If you are trying to buy or rent a home or apartment and you think that you are not treated fairly, you can make a fair housing complaint.

Fair Housing Office
1920 Harper Street, Room 112

Call 555-6001

if you have a problem with housing discrimination.

B Circle the correct answer.

1. An example of a nationality is _____.
   A. Mexican   B. Muslim   c. male

2. An example of a religion is _____.
   A. Mexican   B. Muslim   c. male

3. _____ is an example of family status.
   A. Female   B. Single mother   c. Chinese

4. A person's color could be _____.
   A. green   B. blue   c. black

C Answer the questions about you. Write complete sentences.

1. Do you live in a house or an apartment?

_____

2. Do you rent or own your home?

_____

3. Was it easy to find a good place to live?

_____

4. What problems do you sometimes have with your home?

_____

D Look at the phone book. Match the problems and phone numbers.

CITY OF CARLTON			
AMBULANCE	555-1000	LIBRARY	
ANIMAL CONTROL	555-1100	Main	555-2100
BIRTH RECORDS	555-9000	South	555-2200
GARBAGE, YARD WASTE	555-5000	NOISE COMPLAINTS	555-6700
HEALTH DEPT	555-6000	PARKS	555-4000
HOSPITALS		POISON CONTROL	555-5555
Mercy	555-5200	POLICE	555-8000
Central	555-9000	SCHOOLS	555-3000
HOUSING		SEWAGE	555-9700
Fair Housing Office	555-6001	TRANSIT AUTHORITY	555-7000
Housing Assistance	555-6002	WATER LEAKS	555-9400
MAYOR'S OFFICE	555-2000		

Problems	**Phone Numbers to Call**
1. housing discrimination	a. 555-6700
2. neighbors are noisy	b. 555-9400
3. water leaking in your house or yard	c. 555-6001
4. a dog in your yard	d. 555-1000
5. a medical emergency	e. 555-1100

★ ★

TAKE IT OUTSIDE: Look in your local phone book. Phone numbers for city, state, and federal services are often in the blue section of the phone book. Write the phone numbers for your community.

Animal control: _____   Noise problems: _____

Garbage, trash pickup: _____   Water leaks: _____

Housing discrimination: _____   Poison control: _____

★ ★

Practice Test

DIRECTIONS: Look at the ads to answer the next 5 questions. Use the Answer Sheet.

1 For Sale Condo, 3 bed, 2 bath, pool, garage	2 House For Rent 4 bed, 2.5 bath, garage, nr schools and shopping
3 For Rent Large, sunny apt., near downtown 2 bedrooms, 1 bath, no pets $650/month	4 For Rent Beautiful House 5 bed, 3 bath, patio gar., pool $1200/month

1. Which ad is for an apartment?

   A. 1

   B. 2

   C. 3

   D. 4

2. Which ad is for a condo?

   A. 1

   B. 2

   C. 3

   D. 4

3. Which ad has 3 bathrooms?

   A. 1

   B. 2

   C. 3

   D. 4

4. Which ad has four bedrooms?

   A. 1

   B. 2

   C. 3

   D. 4

5. Which ad has a patio?

   A. 1

   B. 2

   C. 3

   D. 4

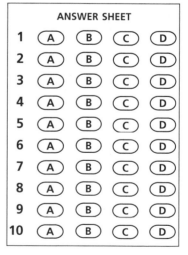

ANSWER SHEET

1	Ⓐ	Ⓑ	Ⓒ	Ⓓ
2	Ⓐ	Ⓑ	Ⓒ	Ⓓ
3	Ⓐ	Ⓑ	Ⓒ	Ⓓ
4	Ⓐ	Ⓑ	Ⓒ	Ⓓ
5	Ⓐ	Ⓑ	Ⓒ	Ⓓ
6	Ⓐ	Ⓑ	Ⓒ	Ⓓ
7	Ⓐ	Ⓑ	Ⓒ	Ⓓ
8	Ⓐ	Ⓑ	Ⓒ	Ⓓ
9	Ⓐ	Ⓑ	Ⓒ	Ⓓ
10	Ⓐ	Ⓑ	Ⓒ	Ⓓ

DIRECTIONS: Look at the phone book listings to answer the next 5 questions. Use the Answer Sheet on page 134.

CITY OF CARLTON FREQUENTLY CALLED NUMBERS			
AMBULANCE	555-1000	LIBRARY	
ANIMAL CONTROL	555-1100	Main	555-2100
BIRTH RECORDS	555-9000	Market Street	555-2300
GARBAGE, YARD WASTE	555-5000	Plaza	555-2400
HEALTH DEPT	555-6000	NOISE COMPLAINTS	555-6700
HOSPITALS		PARKS	555-4444
Mercy	555-5200	POISON CONTROL	555-5555
Central	555-9000	POLICE	555-8000
HOUSING		SCHOOLS	555-3000
Fair Housing Office	555-6001	SEWAGE	555-9700
Housing Assistance	555-6002	TRANSIT AUTHORITY	555-7000
MAYOR'S OFFICE	555-2000	WATER LEAKS	555-9400

6. What number should you call to find out if the Plaza library is open on Sundays?
   - A. 555-2000
   - B. 555-2100
   - C. 555-2200
   - D. 555-2400

7. You want to report a problem with housing discrimination. What number should you call?
   - A. 555-6000
   - B. 555-6001
   - C. 555-6002
   - D. 555-5100

8. You have noisy neighbors. They have a big party every Friday night. What number should you call?
   - A. 555-8000
   - B. 555-6700
   - C. 555-3000
   - D. 555-1000

9. Your next-door neighbor has a dog. The dog is loose and in your yard. What number should you call?
   - A. 555-1000
   - B. 555-1100
   - C. 555-9000
   - D. 555-2200

10. What number should you call if you want your trash picked up?
    - A. 555-1000
    - B. 555-1100
    - C. 555-5000
    - D. 555-2200

HOW DID YOU DO? Count the number of correct answers on your answer sheet. Record this number in the bar graph on the inside back cover.

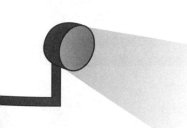

Spotlight: Grammar

SIMPLE PAST STATEMENTS		
Regular verbs	**Irregular verbs**	**Verb** *be*
I He She It You We They } **worked** yesterday. **didn't work** last week.	I He She It You We They } **went** by plane. **didn't go** by train.	I He She It } **was** in class yesterday. **wasn't** at home. You We They } **were** in class yesterday. **weren't** at home.

A Write about yesterday.

1. I cook rice every day.

   _____ yesterday.

2. My sister cleans the house every day.

   _____ yesterday.

3. My teacher runs 40 minutes every day.

   _____ yesterday.

4. The Hermans wash their car every day.

   _____ yesterday.

5. He drinks apple juice every day.

   _____ yesterday.

B Complete the sentences. Use the simple past of the verbs in parentheses.

1. I _____ (walk) to class yesterday. I _____ (not drive).

2. He _____ (get up) at 6 yesterday. He _____ (not sleep) late.

3. We _____ (not go) to class last week. It _____ (be) vacation.

4. They _____ (not work) last Friday. They _____ (spend) the day at the beach.

5. She _____ (eat) a lot at dinner, but she _____ (not drink) anything.

Irregular Verbs	
buy	bought
come	came
cost	cost
drink	drank
eat	ate
get up	got up
go	went
have	had
hurt	hurt
is/are	was/were
leave	left
make	made
meet	met
run	ran
see	saw
sleep	slept
spend	spent

INFORMATION QUESTIONS WITH THE SIMPLE PAST		
What		you eat for breakfast?
Where		we meet them?
When		they leave for work?
Why	**did**	she leave yesterday?
Who		he meet at the party?
How much bread		your children eat yesterday?
How many apples		they eat yesterday?

C Match the questions and answers.

Questions	Answers
1. What did you do last Monday?	_____ They were on sale.
2. Why did you buy bananas last week?	___1___ I went to school and to work.
3. How many did you buy?	_____ We ate at home.
4. When did you go to bed last night?	_____ I watched about 2 hours.
5. Who did you write to last month?	_____ I went to bed at 10:00 P.M.
6. Where did you eat dinner last night?	_____ I bought 12.
7. How much TV did you watch yesterday?	_____ I wrote to my parents.

D Answer the questions about you.

1. What did you do yesterday?

_____

2. When did you get up today?

_____

3. Where did you go last Saturday?

_____

4. Who did you see last night?

_____

LESSON 1

Can you use a computer?

A Match the jobs and actions.

Jobs

1. chef __i__
2. child care worker _____
3. construction worker _____
4. stylist _____
5. landscaper _____
6. mechanic _____
7. mover _____
8. office manager _____
9. plumber _____
10. truck driver _____

Actions

a. takes care of children
b. takes care of plants
c. uses a computer
d. drives a truck
e. lifts heavy things
f. builds buildings
g. fixes cars
h. repairs toilets
i. cooks food
j. cuts hair

B Read the story. Answer the questions.

Claire is 16 years old. She is looking for a job. She wants to work after school. Claire can drive a car. She got her driver's license last month. She can take care of children. She took care of her sister's children for a week last year. Claire is in 11th grade. She learned to use a computer in school.

1. What 3 things can Claire do?

_____

2. Does Claire want a full-time job?

_____

3. What job(s) do you think Claire can do?

_____

C Answer the questions about you.

1. What 3 things can you do?

   _____

2. What kind of job do you want in the future?

   _____

3. Do you want to work 40 hours a week?

   _____

D Write about you. Use your answers in Activity C to write a paragraph.

_____

_____

_____

E Circle the correct answer.

1. Did Tony wash the car yesterday?
   - Ⓐ Yes, he did.
   - B. No, they didn't.

2. Did you clean the kitchen?
   - A. Yes, I did.
   - B. No, you didn't.

3. Did you and Sam go to the store last week?
   - A. Yes, they did.
   - B. No, we didn't.

4. Did you eat with your sister yesterday?
   - A. Yes, she did.
   - B. No, I didn't.

5. Did he work last week?
   - A. Yes, he did.
   - B. No, they didn't.

6. Did they go out last night?
   - A. Yes, they did.
   - B. No, we didn't.

2 **LESSON**

Do you have experience?

A Write the abbreviations next to the words.

FT	PT	eves.	hr.	exp.	✓ req'd

1. required   _____req'd_____
2. hour   _____
3. evenings   _____
4. full-time   _____
5. experience   _____
6. part-time   _____

B Read the ads. Complete the sentences.

FT Office Manager
Professional and
friendly person
needed for busy
office. Exp. req'd.
Computer and office
skills req'd. Benefits.
$400/week. Fax resume
to: (704) 555-9702

Landscaper
Exp'd FT landscaper
needed. Driver's
license req'd. $18/hr.
Good benefits.
Apply in person to:
Parker Homes
112 North Ave.
Leesburg, VA.

Stylist
PT stylist
needed, eves. 1 year
exp. preferred. $8.50/hr
Call Angie:
(617) 555-2234

1. The _____office manager_____ needs to have office skills.
2. The two full-time jobs are for an _____ and a _____.
3. The _____ job is part-time.
4. Experience is preferred for the _____.
5. The _____ job is in the evening.
6. The landscaper job pays _____ an hour.
7. You need computer skills for the _____ job.
8. You need a _____ for the landscaper job.
9. If you want to apply for the _____ job, you need to go in person to the office.
10. If you want to apply for the _____ job, you need to call Angie.
11. If you want to apply for the _____ job, you need to fax a resume.

C Take notes on the ads on page 140. Complete the chart.

JOB	FT OR PT	$	WHAT IS REQUIRED	HOW TO APPLY
office manager				Fax resume
		$18/hour		
	Part-time			Call

D Answer the questions.

1. Mark got the landscaper job in Activity B. How much does he earn in one week working 40 hours?

   _____

2. Mark gets an extra $9 ($18 + $9) an hour when he works on Saturdays.
   How much does he earn for 8 hours on a Saturday?

   _____

3. Tony wants to be an office manager. How much money does the office manager earn in one hour?

   _____

4. Julia got the job as a stylist. How much money will she earn for 10 hours of work?

   _____

5. Angie works with Julia, but she makes $3 more an hour.
   How much does Angie earn in 10 hours?

   _____

E Put the conversation in order. Number the sentences from first (1) to last (5).

_____ Do you have experience?

_____ Can you come in for an interview tomorrow at 10?

_____ Yes, I do. I was a mechanic for 3 years in Mexico.

___1___ I'm calling about the ad for a mechanic.

_____ Yes. I'll be there at 10.

3
LESSON

Tell me about yourself.

A Match the questions and answers.

Interviewer's Questions

1. Where are you working now?
2. Do you like your job?
3. What did you do before that?
4. When was that?
5. Did you like that job?
6. Do you have experience?

Job Applicant's Answers

a. Yes, I was an office manager for 2 years.
b. Not really. It's not very interesting.
c. At BigMart.
d. Yes, very much. The people were nice, and I learned to use a computer.
e. I was a salesclerk at Best Books.
f. From April, 2003 to January, 2005.

B Answer the questions about you.

1. Are you working now?

   _____

2. What did you do before?

   _____

3. When was that?

   _____

4. Do you have experience as an office manager?

   _____

5. What skills do you have? (for example, *I can drive a truck*.)

   _____

C Where do you think they work? Write the jobs next to the places on page 143.

stylist	construction worker	landscaper
child care worker	chef	plumber
mover	mechanic	truck driver

1. A-1 Trucking   _____
2. Caring for Kids   _____
3. Anthony's Italian Restaurant   _____
4. Green Thumb Landscaping   _____
5. National Moving Company   _____

D Read the job interview tips. Check *true* or *false* below.

www.howtogetajob.com

HOME
TIPS
EMAIL

Interview Tips

- Dress appropriately.
- Arrive early.
- Bring paper and a pen.
- Know the name of the interviewer and how to pronounce it.
- Be polite to everyone.
- Do not chew gum or smoke.
- Ask questions if you don't understand something.
- Wait 1–2 seconds before you answer a question.

In a job interview,

1. you should wear dirty clothes.	☐ true	☑ false
2. you should smoke if you want to.	☐ true	☐ false
3. you shouldn't chew gum.	☐ true	☐ false
4. you should ask questions.	☐ true	☐ false
5. you should wait a little before you answer.	☐ true	☐ false
6. you shouldn't call the interviewer by name.	☐ true	☐ false

LESSON 4

The Amazing Story of Mr. Nichols

A Learn new words. Find and underline the words in the story.

married	got his first job	died
started racing motorcycles	became owner	decided to go back to school
started teaching	was born	finished college

OBITUARIES   August 10, 2004

Mr. Douglas Nichols, 65, of Fort Henry, died August 9, 2004 at Mercy South Hospital. He was born December 22, 1939 in Pine Bluff, Arkansas, the son of Lewis and Maria Nichols. He lived in Fort Henry from 1978 until his death. He married Sophia Wasawski in 1964.

Early in life, Doug showed great mechanical ability. He could fix watches in first grade. As he got older, he started to fix cars, airplanes, and motorcycles.

He got his first job as a motorcycle mechanic in 1958. In 1966, Doug became the owner of the Nichols Motorcycle Company. He wasn't happy just fixing motorcycles, he wanted to ride them, too. He started racing motorcycles in 1965. Doug also loved boats, and began racing speed boats in 1967. He set a world speed boat record in Florida in 1971.

When Doug was 50 years old, he decided to go back to school. He finished college in 1994. He started teaching science in 1995 and continued until 2002.

Survivors include his wife, Sophia, and sons, Ivan and Gregory.

B Number the events from first (1) to last (6).

_____ Douglas Nichols died.

_____ Doug got his first job.

_1_ He was born.

_____ He married Sophia.

_____ Doug became the owner of Nichols Motorcycle Company.

_____ He finished college.

C Write the events from the box on page 144 on the timeline below.

1939	_____
1958	_____
1964	_____
1966	_____
1989	_____
1994	_____
1995	_____
2004	_____

D Complete the timeline for you. Write when you were born and other important things.

_____	_____
_____	_____
_____	_____
_____	_____
_____	_____

E Complete the sentences. Write *am, is,* or *are.*

1. I _____*am*_____ going to apply for a job.

2. She _____ going to help me with my application.

3. _____ he going to call you today?

4. The students _____ going to go to the library tomorrow.

5. Do you think it _____ going to rain tonight?

6. _____ you going to finish college?

F Write 3 things you are going to do in the next year. Use *am going to* in your sentences.

_____

_____

_____

What are your goals?

A Take the quiz.

What are your goals for the future?

Check the things you would like to do in the next 5 years.

☐ get married   ☐ spend more time with family

☐ have a child   ☐ go to another country

☐ start college   ☐ buy a car

☐ get a better job   ☐ buy a house

☐ learn to speak   ☐ read more books
English better

☐ meet new people

☐ _____

_____ (your idea)

B Read the story. Underline Tatiana's goals.

Tatiana is from Peru. She came to the United States in 1999 with her daughter, Claudia. Tatiana is working in a clothing store now and Claudia goes to school. Tatiana loves to cook and wants to be a chef. She wants to work in a nice restaurant, so she is going to start classes at the community college in September. She is going to study how to be a chef. Tatiana is saving money for her classes. She needs $1,000. Tatiana is going to work some extra hours at the store, but she wants Claudia to have child care after school. Tatiana is going to ask her sister to take care of Claudia after school.

C Complete the chart.

TATIANA'S GOAL	WHAT TATIANA IS GOING TO DO TO REACH HER GOAL
Be a chef	
	Work extra hours at the store
Have child care for Claudia	

D Choose 3 of your goals from Activity A. Write them in the chart.

YOUR GOAL	HOW MUCH $ IT WILL COST	WHAT YOU ARE GOING TO DO TO REACH YOUR GOAL

★ ★

TAKE IT OUTSIDE: Interview a family member, friend, or coworker. Ask the questions. Complete the chart.

Name: _____

WHAT ARE 2 GOALS YOU HAVE FOR THE NEXT YEAR?	HOW MUCH MONEY WILL IT COST?	WHAT IS 1 THING YOU WILL DO TO REACH YOUR GOAL?

★ ★

What is the minimum wage?

A Predict the answers to the questions below. Match the questions and answers.

Questions

1. What is the minimum wage?
2. When is overtime due?
3. What is the youngest age that a person can work?
4. What is the minimum wage if the worker receives tips?

Answers

a. $2.13
b. $5.15
c. for more than 40 hours in a work week
d. 14 years for most types of work

B Read these Frequently Asked Questions (FAQs). Check your predictions in Activity A.

U.S. Department of Labor

www.dol.gov/elaws

Search / A-Z Index

By topic I By audience I By top 20 requested items I By form I By organization I By location

March 27, 2005

e**laws** - Frequently Asked Questions

WAGES, PAY, AND BENEFITS

1. **What is the minimum wage?** The federal minimum wage for employees is $5.15 per hour.
2. **What is the minimum wage for workers who receive tips?** An employer of a tipped employee is only required to pay $2.13 an hour in wages if that amount plus the tips received equals at least the federal minimum wage.
3. **Do young workers need to be paid the minimum wage?** The federal minimum wage is $5.15 per hour. However, a special minimum wage of $4.25 per hour applies to employees under the age of 20 during their first 90 calendar days of employment with an employer.

OVERTIME AND WORK HOURS

4. **When is overtime due?** The Fair Labor Standards Act (FLSA) requires overtime pay at a rate of not less than one and one-half times an employee's regular rate of pay after 40 hours of work in a workweek.

CHILD LABOR

5. **What is the youngest age at which a person can be employed?** The Fair Labor Standards Act (FLSA) sets 14 as the minimum age for most non-farm work. However, at any age, youth can deliver newspapers; perform in radio, television, movie, or theatrical productions; work in businesses owned by their parents; and baby-sit or perform minor chores around a private home.

C Write the number of the question in Activity B where you can find the answer.

1. Can a 12-year-old baby-sit? _____Question 5_____

2. How much is overtime pay? _____

3. Do 16-year-old workers have to get $5.15 an hour? _____

4. Waiters in restaurants get tips. What is the minimum wage for waiters? _____

5. What is "overtime"? _____

6. How old do you have to be for most jobs? _____

D Check *true* or *false*.

1. The information in Activity B can be found on the computer.

   ☑ true   ☐ false

2. An FAQ is a Frequently Asked Question.

   ☐ true   ☐ false

3. Workers in the United States need to get $7.50 or more for an hour of work.

   ☐ true   ☐ false

4. You can't get information about laws in the United States by using the computer.

   ☐ true   ☐ false

5. The Fair Labor Standards Act is a law that tells people about work, wages, and hours.

   ☐ true   ☐ false

6. You can probably get this information at the library.

   ☐ true   ☐ false

★ ★

TAKE IT OUTSIDE: Find a computer (at a library or computer lab if you don't have one). Go to the website www.dol.gov/elaws/faq. Write down 2 FAQs and the answers. Ask a librarian, lab instructor, or other student for help if you need it.

Question: _____

Answer: _____

Question: _____

Answer: _____

★ ★

Practice Test

DIRECTIONS: Look at the ads to answer the next 5 questions. Use the Answer Sheet.

A.

Child Care Worker
FT or PT. M-F, 7 a.m. – 5 p.m.,
no exp. req'd. Need responsible
and friendly person.
Apply in person:
Tiny Toddlers
1619 West Avenue

B.

Chef
Mario's Pizzeria
Full-time, 3–11,
Tuesdays–Saturdays
1 year exp. req'd.
To apply, call:
(202) 555-6200
Ask for Tham.

C.

Plumbers and helpers
needed with experience
for new company. FT.
Great pay, benefits.
Driver's license req'd.
Call (608) 555-7925.

D.

Landscaper
FT landscaper needed
at Health Inc. 7 a.m. to 3:30.
Benefits. 2 years min.
exp. Apply in person,
1900 Selwyn Rd.

ANSWER SHEET				
1	A	B	C	D
2	A	B	C	D
3	A	B	C	D
4	A	B	C	D
5	A	B	C	D
6	A	B	C	D
7	A	B	C	D
8	A	B	C	D
9	A	B	C	D
10	A	B	C	D

1. Tina needs a part-time job. Which one is good for her?

   A. Job A

   B. Job B

   C. Job C

   D. Job D

2. Which job is in the evenings?

   A. Job A

   B. Job B

   C. Job C

   D. Job D

3. Which job includes great pay?

   A. Job A

   B. Job B

   C. Job C

   D. Job D

4. John has to go to class at 4. Which job ends before then?

   A. child care worker

   B. chef

   C. plumber

   D. landscaper

5. Which job does **not** require experience?

   A. child care worker

   B. chef

   C. plumber

   D. landscaper

DIRECTIONS: Look at the job application to answer the next 5 questions. Use the Answer Sheet on page 150.

Job Application Form
(PLEASE PRINT)

First Name _____ Middle Initial _____ ①

Last Name _____ ②

Birth Date ___6/23/70_____

Present Address _____ ③

City _____ State _____ Zip Code __95652__

Phone Number ___(916)555-4938_____

- Are you currently employed? ☐ Yes ☐ No ④
- Do you have a valid driver's license? ☑ Yes ☐ No ⑤
- Do you have access to an automobile? ☑ Yes ☐ No

- Number of hours/week desired: _____ ⑥
- Days & A.M./P.M. hours available:

	Mon.	Tues.	Wed.	Thurs.	Fri.	Sat.	Sun.
A.M.	☑	☑	☑	☑	☑	☑	☐
P.M.	☐	☐	☐	☐	☐	☐	☐

⑦

---

6. On what line do you write your first name?
   A. Line 1   C. Line 3
   B. Line 2   D. Line 4

7. On what line should you write your address?
   A. Line 1   C. Line 3
   B. Line 2   D. Line 4

8. Lidia is working now, but she wants a new job. Where does she say this?
   A. Line 1   C. Line 3
   B. Line 2   D. Line 4

9. Ben can only work on Wednesday and Thursday nights. Where does he say this?
   A. Line 4   C. Line 6
   B. Line 5   D. Line 7

10. Where do you check that you have a driver's license?
   A. Line 4   C. Line 6
   B. Line 5   D. Line 7

HOW DID YOU DO? Count the number of correct answers on your answer sheet. Record this number in the bar graph on the inside back cover.

Correlation Table

Student Book Pages	Workbook Pages
Pre-Unit	
2–3	
Unit 1	
4–5	2–3
6–7	4–5
8–9	6–7
10–11	8–9
12–13	
14–15	10–13
16–17	14–15
18–19	16–17
Unit 2	
20–21	18–19
22–23	20–21
24–25	22–23
26–27	24–25
28–29	
30–31	26–29
32–33	30–31
34–35	
Unit 3	
36–37	32–33
38–39	34–35
40–41	36–37
42–43	38–39
44–45	
46–47	40–43
48–49	44–45
50–51	46–47

Student Book Pages	Workbook Pages
Unit 4	
52–53	48–49
54–55	50–51
56–57	52–53
58–59	54–55
60–61	
62–63	56–59
64–65	60–61
66–67	
Unit 5	
68–69	62–63
70–71	64–65
72–73	66–67
74–75	68–69
76–77	
78–79	70–73
80–81	74–75
82–83	76–77
Unit 6	
84–85	78–79
86–87	80–81
88–89	82–83
90–91	84–85
92–93	
94–95	86–89
96–97	90–91
98–99	

Student Book Pages	Workbook Pages		Student Book Pages	Workbook Pages
Unit 7			**Unit 9**	
100–101	92–93		132–133	122–123
102–103	94–95		134–135	124–125
104–105	96–97		136–137	126–127
106–107	98–99		138–139	128–129
108–109			140–141	
110–111	100–103		142–143	130–133
112–113	104–105		144–145	134–135
114–115	106–107		146–147	136–137
Unit 8			**Unit 10**	
116–117	108–109		148–149	138–139
118–119	110–111		150–151	140–141
120–121	112–113		152–153	142–143
122–123	114–115		154–155	144–145
124–125			156–157	
126–127	116–119		158–159	146–149
128–129	120–121		160–161	150–151
130–131			162–163	